Also by Neil Zurcher:

Neil Zurcher's Favorite One Tank Trips
More of Neil Zurcher's One Tank Trips
One Tank Trips Road Food

Neil Zurcher

A GUIDE TO THE CURIOUS ATTRACTIONS OF THE BUCKEYE STATE

GRAY & COMPANY, PUBLISHERS
CLEVELAND

This book is dedicated to my wife, Bonnie

to my kids,
Melody and Ernie McCallister
Melissa and Peter Luttmann
Craig W. Zurcher

to my grandkids,
Allison and Bryan McCallister
Ryan and Jason Luttmann

and to Lowell Gatts,
a teacher, who became my friend, and taught me to be curious.
A man who believed I could achieve things when others did not.
A man who made a difference in young lives, but, whose own
life ended much too soon.

© 2001 by Neil Zurcher

Photo credits appear on page 208

Gray & Company, Publishers
1588 East 40th Street
Cleveland, Ohio 44103-2302
(216) 431-2665
www.grayco.com

This guide was prepared on the basis of the author's best knowledge at the time of publication. However, because of constantly changing conditions beyond his control, the author disclaims any responsibility for the accuracy and completeness of the information in this guide. Users of this guide are cautioned not to place undue reliance upon the validity of the information contained herein and to use this guide at their own risk.

ISBN 1-886228-49-3

Printed in the United States of America

Third printing

CONTENTS

INTRODUCTION

When I was very young it was the time of the Great Depression and my family, like lots of families then, was just scraping by. We lived with my mother's parents, and my father was an executive with an insurance company. But with the Depression not many people were buying insurance.

For entertainment, we took lots of car rides. My father was always interested in the curious, the unusual. The first trip I recall was to Pymatuning Lake, just across the Pennsylvania border, where people fed day-old bread to the hungry carp. The carp were so numerous that the water would literally boil as thousands of fish would fight for a bread crust tossed from the shore. There were also wild ducks and geese on the lake and they would try to get into the act too. It was quite a sight, watching ducks and geese literally walk on the backs of the fish as all competed for the bread.

Then there was the "Blue Hole" in Castalia, Ohio. That one I didn't understand too well when I was very young. All I could see was a pond filled with blue-green water. No fish, nothing moved, I thought it was pretty boring. My father assured me that this was a special place because the "hole" had no bottom, that, according to early brochures horses and cows had fallen in and never been seen again, sucked into some kind of underground river. Well, that made it a little more interesting, and besides there was a trout stream beside it where you could get a box of popcorn and feed the fish. (We did a lot of fish feeding during those years.)

My father loved to call my attention to the biggest, the smallest, the one-and-only of anything he had seen or read about.

My favorite spot of all the wild and wonderful curious spots we would seek out was in Mitawanga, Ohio, west of Vermilion. A man had an electric train set that he had built into his back yard. He called it "Miniature City," and it was about the size of half a tennis court. It was a magic place for little kids. The trains ran in and out of real mountains that he had made of dirt. The little river that ran through the town was real water, and the tiny homes had electric lights and real grass lawns. Everything was in perfect scale, including the tiny cannonballs stacked by a miniature Civil War cannon in a park. There were sound effects and music, and for a nickel (or maybe it was a dime), you could stay as long as you wanted. I found it especially magical after dark, when you could walk under the stars and feel like Gulliver discovering the land of the Lilliputians.

As a reporter for nearly half a century, I have had plenty of opportunities to continue discovering wonderful little curiosities around the state—many of them that might not make the news but that did get a scribble in the back of my reporter's notebook to remind me that someday I should visit them again and perhaps tell their story.

I don't think that any one section of Ohio has more claim to being the oddest part of the state. I'm sure that there will be more things listed here from the northern part of Ohio, because that's where I live, and I've been exposed to more things here. But I have been travelling Ohio, all of Ohio, for my "One Tank Trips" television segments for more than 20 years, and I've learned that Weird can be found almost anyplace. Strange is no stranger to Ohio. From a headless rooster that wouldn't die in Ashtabula County in the northeast corner to the "Hollow Earth theory" expounded by a man in Southwest Ohio. From bottle feeding carp in the Muskingum River in Southeast Ohio to a twelve-hole brick privy on the National Register of Historic places in Northwest Ohio. In Central Ohio I found the little chicken who bought his own lunch every day.

No matter where you live in our wonderful state, you will find idiosyncrasies, curiosities, and oddities. I hope that perhaps this book will "prime the well" and that you'll let me know about things I may have missed so that every couple of years I can bring this book up to date with the new wondrous and weird things that make the Buckeyes State such an interesting place.

OHiO Oddities™

CENTRAL

The First Traffic Light

ASHVILLE

The next time you zip through a red light, you might remember a couple of Ohioans who were responsible for that signal.

Garrett A. Morgan, of Cleveland, was the first person to apply to the U.S. Patent Office for a patent on such a device. Morgan's worked this way. It was a T-shaped pole unit that featured three positions: stop, go, and an all-directional stop position. The third position was used to allow pedestrians to cross safely. While technically not a light, this traffic signal led to further inventions.

Teddy Boor, of Ashville, invented and built the nation's oldest working traffic *light*. It was installed in downtown Ashville, south of Columbus. This odd-looking unit offered red and green lights with a slowly rotating hand that would sweep across each bulb, letting drivers know how much time was left before the light would change. The bullet-shaped light hung at the corner of Main Street and Long Street for more than 50 years, until finally the state transportation department made the community take it down and replace it with a more modern signal.

The village obeyed, but saved their piece of history in the **Ashville Museum** (34 Long St., Ashville; 740-983-9864), where it still stops and starts visitors.

The Chicken Who Bought His Own Lunch
ASHVILLE

In Ashville, they still talk about the chicken who bought his own lunch. His name was Chic-Chic, and as chickens go he was pretty small. Actually, he was a bantam rooster, which means that even full grown he barely topped six inches from his feet to the top of his rooster comb. But Chic-Chic was a giant in his own mind.

He belonged to a local widow, who lived just around the corner from a restaurant. Every day the woman would put a dime in Chic-Chic's beak and tell him to go to the restaurant and get his food.

The little bird, dime clenched tightly in his beak, would strut down to the corner, make a left on Long Street, and continue strutting right down the middle of the sidewalk, forcing humans to give way as he made his way to the front step of the restaurant. There he would deposit the dime and stand, clucking, until the owner brought out a Ball jar cap filled with corn and set it down for Chic-Chic to eat from.

Jack Lemon, a volunteer at the Ashville Museum, remembers Chic-Chic well. "That little bird would make that trip every day, winter or summer, rain or shine," he said.

And when he was done eating, Chic-Chic would wander over to the bus stop to greet visitors from other towns. No one knew how he did it, but he always seemed to know just when a bus was due, and he would be there to cluck at the arrivals.

"He just thought he owned this town," former mayor and now museum curator, Charlie Morrison told me. "Everybody knew him, everybody loved him."

Today Chic-Chic and his owner are gone. (Chic-Chic died back in the 1950s), but there's a model of the little guy, with a dime in his beak, in the **Ashville Museum** (34 Long St., Ashville; 740-983-9864).

"He just thought he owned this town.
Everybody knew him, everybody loved him."

The Tragedy of the Shenandoah

AVA

The *Shenandoah* was big. Almost 700 feet long. (Picture a Great Lakes ore boat—in the air!) She was America's first airship, or dirigible—an aircraft that resembled a blimp, but with a rigid frame inside, and far bigger than any blimp in the sky today.

"Shenandoah" is a Native American word that supposedly means "daughter of the stars." Her official name was ZR-1, for "Zeppelin, Ridged, 1." She was born at Lakehurst, New Jersey, where she was assembled in 1923.

In truth, the navy wasn't exactly sure how to use her. She did badly in the first navy war games in which she participated. She was too big a target and moved too slowly to escape being tracked by anti-aircraft guns.

But while the navy seemed uncertain, the public loved her. Traffic on the highways would come to a halt as the huge ship flew over a town or village. People would pour out of their homes and schools to point skyward.

The *Shenandoah* was the first airship to fly nonstop coast to coast. With five huge Packard engines and a range of five thousand miles without landing, she was the wonder of her day. It appeared that her future would be doing public relations for the navy.

She was doing just that, making a publicity flight in September of 1925, when she hit a giant thunderstorm over Ava, Ohio.

There is some speculation that it was "wind shear" that tore the great ship in half.

The control car plummeted to the ground, narrowly missing a farmhouse, and killing the airship commander, Zachary Landsdowne, and several of his crew. The rear of the ship flew on about another mile before it, too, sagged to earth, killing several of the crew trapped aboard that section but sparing the lives of several others.

By far the most dramatic part of the crash was what happened to the front of the dirigible. The undamaged helium-filled bags began carrying that part of the ship, with seven people still trapped alive inside, back up into the storm.

Then a downdraft caught it as it floated over the Ernest Nichols farm (on what is today Ohio Route 78). Nichols, who had been alerted by neighbors, was standing beside his house when the huge floating hulk headed out of the clouds toward his home.

Voices from the apparition screamed at him to grab a rope and tie it down. He quickly grabbed one of the dangling lines and wrapped it around a fence post. A second later a slight updraft yanked the fence post out of the ground.

The voices from above were still imploring him to tie down one of the dangling ropes, so he wrapped a couple of them around some tree stumps, which held. Moments later, men slid down the ropes out of the floating bag.

Six were uninjured, a seventh was snatched from the bag when it brushed a tree. He fell to the ground, unconscious but alive.

Among the survivors was Lieutenant Commander Charles Rosendahl, the navigator, who asked the gathering farmers for shotguns. He wanted to shoot down the bag before it could drift off and do any further damage.

Shotguns appeared, and volley after volley was fired into the still airborne gasbags. They finally sank to the ground in farmer Nichols's yard, and the *Shenandoah*'s last flight was over.

Fourteen were dead, but, miraculously, 29 escaped alive.

For days and weeks tiny Ava, Ohio, only a wide spot on the highway, was in the national headlines. People came from all over to gawk and stare at the three crash sites. Then slowly the disaster faded out of the news and became a footnote in the history of aviation. No Hollywood movies were made about the dramatic crash. The *Shenandoah* was pretty much forgotten, except in Noble County.

Take Bryan and Theresa Rayner, of Ava. They bill themselves as collectors and historians of the *USS Shenandoah*. Bryan runs the family business, Rayner's Garage and Towing. Theresa works at the Ava post office. Together they have amassed hundreds of pictures and artifacts from the crash—parts of the ill-fated ship, and things like a bottle of sugar cubes that was once in the *Shenandoah*'s galley. They even have what may have been the world's first bumper sticker, a paper sticker that boasted, "I've seen the *Shenandoah* crash site!" In short they have created their own unusual museum honoring the navy's first airship.

All of their treasures are stored in a banged-up camper trailer that Bryan rescued from a rollover on nearby Interstate 77. The **mobile museum** (50495 State Rte. 821, Ava; 740-732-2624) usually sits in front of Rayner's Garage, but they occasionally take it to nearby schools to give programs on Noble County history and the *Shenandoah*.

They don't have regular hours, but Bryan says visitors are welcome to go through the trailer anytime he's around, or they can stop in at the Ava post office and see if Theresa is available to give them a tour. There is no charge, but they do accept donations to help them add to their collection.

You can also see the site where the rear portion of the airship crashed to earth, located beside I-77 near the Caldwell exit. Just look on the west side of the highway for a ravine and a flag, a sign, and lots of stones that outline where the disabled craft landed.

The Rayners can give you directions to the other two crash sites.

The Shenandoah collection is stored in a banged-up camper trailer that Bryan rescued from a rollover on nearby I-77.

One Speedy Pumpkin Carver

BALTIMORE

Jerry Ayers of Baltimore, Ohio, is not a man to trifle with when he has a knife in his hand. He can carve up a face in literally seconds.

Jerry, you see, is one of the world's fastest pumpkin carvers.

It wasn't a lifelong goal. Jerry was once a real-estate salesman, but his hobby of carving pumpkins for his kids and grandkids kept getting in the way.

Jerry had found that by designing his own carving knife, a long thin blade, he could carve out the face of a jack-o'-lantern faster than

anyone he knew. So when TV station WCMH in Columbus challenged him to carve a pumpkin on their live show one morning, he took the challenge and set an unofficial world record—1 minute and 56 seconds! And it wasn't your normal saw-toothed, triangle-eyed jack-o'-lantern. His finished product was a series of graceful swirls and arches that created a face with eyes and eyebrows, a distinctive nose, and a mouth that was a work of art. Jerry had found a new career.

In 1999, he entered the *Guinness Book of World Records* as the world's fastest pumpkin carver. He carved a "very detailed jack-o'-lantern" in 1 minute and 37 seconds. On the day he set that record, he set a second one by carving more than a ton of pumpkins in just 7 hours and 11 minutes. The following year he broke his own single-pumpkin record with a time of 1 minute and 18 seconds in an appearance on CBS's *Saturday Early Show* in New York.

Jerry now sells his knives and his pumpkin face designs under the name of "Designer Pumpkins" in grocery stores all over the country and on the Internet. And, yes, he still carves his own jack-o'-lanterns each Halloween at his home in Baltimore.

The Greatest Pumpkin

CIRCLEVILLE

Linus should have looked for The Great Pumpkin in the town of Circleville, home to the "Greatest Free Show on Earth"—the Circleville Pumpkin Show, always held on the third weekend in October.

And they like their pumpkins big. One recent first-prize winner weighed 528 pounds!

The festival started in 1903, when mayor George R. Haswell decided to hold a small exhibit for Halloween in front of his place on West Main Street. Some corn fodder and carved pumpkins were the decorations. People liked it so much that the following year some merchants added more pumpkins to the exhibit, and it slowly grew into an annual event.

They decided to call it the "Greatest Free Show on Earth." The free part is accurate, at least, because no admission fees are charged. Over the years the show has grown to the sixth-largest festival in the United States and attracts upwards of 300,000 people for its annual four-day run.

Today at the festival you can find not only pumpkins but also anything you can name that is made with pumpkin, from pumpkin pie to pumpkin cookies and pumpkin ice cream. There are parades and beauty contests. For four days in the autumn, pumpkins put Circleville on the map.

A Painting Comes to Life
COLUMBUS

Is it a garden or a picture? Life imitates art imitating life at a park in Columbus, where sculptor James T. Mason created a living replica of Georges Seurat's famous painting *A Sunday Afternoon on the Island of La Grande Jatte* from plants.

Mason got the idea while visiting a botanical garden in Philadelphia where, he said, the gardens and topiaries reminded him of an impressionist painting.

He came back to Columbus and turned the Old Deaf School Park at East Town and Washington Avenue into a living copy of Seurat's masterpiece.

The park now contains 80 life-size topiaries that depict Parisians dressed in their Victorian-era clothing looking at the river Seine.

Mason has created art with yew trees that he trims and shapes to match life-size molds of the figures he wants. The garden painting includes human figures, a boat being rowed on a pond, and three dogs, a cat, and a monkey.

Admission to the park, located only blocks from the Ohio Statehouse, is free.

The Accounting Hall of Fame

COLUMBUS

Who can forget the glory days of Joel Stanley Demski, Shaun Fenton O'Malley, or Ross Macgregor Skinner?

These and other greats are enshrined at Ohio State University. Are they football players? you ask. Baseball stars? Nope. Accountants.

Yes, OSU is home to the **Accounting Hall of Fame** (Fisher College of Business, Ohio State University, 2100 Neil Ave., Columbus; 614-292-9368). It was established in 1950 "for the purpose of honoring accountants who have made, or are making, significant contributions to the advancement of accounting since the beginning of the 20th century."

More than 60 number crunchers have been enshrined. No parades or big hoopla when new members enter, though: just the presentation of a certificate at the annual meeting of the American Accounting Association.

I think the Accounting Hall of Fame should have a gift shop where visitors and accounting fans could go to buy, say, T-shirts with a picture of a ledger book on them, or perhaps with some snappy columnar entries as a graphic. Coffee mugs with . . . well you get the idea.

Butter Cows

COLUMBUS

Rodin was famous for the *Thinker*, Michelangelo for his *David*. Dan Ross, of Columbus, is known for his cow made of butter. He started sculpting the cow in 1963 and created a new one each year for the next 36 years.

The first time I went to the Ohio State Fair I was only 14 years old, but I knew there was one thing I wanted to see. Not the Grand Champion Bull. Not the horse-pulling championship. Not the Hollywood Stage Show. No, what I wanted to see first was the life-size cow made of butter.

I had been hearing about this cow since I was old enough to remember. My grandmother had once gone to the state fair, and her most vivid memory was of a man using buckets of warm butter to mold a dandelion-yellow Holstein. No little bitty cow, this was a full five-foot-tall, six-foot-long cow, right down to the faucets in the back. I figured if it was good enough to impress Grandma, I should see it, too.

I walked into this big hallway, and at the end was a frosted-over window looking into a giant refrigerator. And there she was. Not only was there a life-size butter cow, she even had a life-size, Grade-A butter calf right alongside her.

It was the most curious thing I had ever seen. I was disappointed later to find out that state fairs in other states have also displayed cows made of butter. But how many of them have also displayed Neil Armstrong, John Glenn, and race-car driver Bobby Rahal in 1,500 pounds of butter?

The cow and calf butter sculptures are still featured each year at the **Ohio State Fair** (17th St., Columbus; 888-646-3976).

1,500 pounds of creamy, Grade-A sculpture.

Which Came First, the Whistle or the Pea?

COLUMBUS

The last of its breed, the **American Whistle Corporation** (6540 Huntley Rd., Columbus; 877-876-2380) is the only maker of metal whistles in the United States.

Whistles. You know. Those things that policemen use. Referees and coaches clench them tightly in their jaws. Majorettes and drum majors use them to command bands and flag corps. In fact, the company makes the official NFL referee whistles for the annual Superbowl game.

If you want to see how they make whistles (the big moment is when they squeeze in the little ball of cork), they'll show you around for a fee that includes a whistle when you leave. (They'll then trot you through the company store, where you can buy a commemorative bronze, gold, or silver whistle to present to your favorite coach or policeman.)

What's "Brushstrokes" Got to Do with Flying?

COLUMBUS

During the 1970s, "Pop Art" was all the rage, and the icon of the era was Roy Lichtenstein. By the mid 1980s, the Columbus city council was ready to show they were "with it" and commissioned Lichtenstein to create a modernistic abstract piece for the **Port Columbus Airport** (4600 International Gateway, Columbus, 614-239-4083).

Lichtenstein delivered *Brushstrokes in Flight*, a 25-foot-tall, angular aluminum sculpture with what appear to be giant brush strokes soaring into the sky.

The commissioners were apparently less than overwhelmed by the artwork; they put it in the airport's daily parking lot, where it was spattered by rain, dust, and dirt for many years, with hardly anyone noticing its existence.

In fact, at one point then-mayor Dana "Buck" Rinehart tried to give the sculpture away. He offered it to Columbus's sister city, Genoa, Italy. Maybe Buck just hated the sculpture and wanted it far away from Columbus; maybe he really liked it and was trying to make a big impression with his grandiose offer. Either way, he forgot to ask City Council, which reminded him it was city property and not his to give away. (The fact that at about that time the sculpture was appraised at $750,000 may have had something to do with their decision to keep it.)

The commissioners finally moved the statue out of the weather and inside the terminal to a more dignified location—near the food court. They even built a 8bench around it to keep kids from climbing on it.

Gentlemen, Start Your, Uh . . . Lawn Mowers
COLUMBUS

It started in 1991 with a one-dollar bet between two residents of Dewberry Lane in Columbus who decided to race each other while mowing an elderly neighbor's lawn. The bet was on whose riding mower could get through a swampy part of the lawn the fastest. This was the start of the "Pit," and the formation of the Dewberry Mudboggers Lawnmower Racing Team—the world's only known lawn mower mud-racing team.

The venerable sport of lawn mower racing has, of course, mowed its way across America. Though there's some disagreement about

NEVER GIVE AWAY YOUR GOOD LUCK

Alliance doctor Levi Lamborn liked flowers. He especially liked carnations. He even developed a special breed of scarlet carnation, of which he was so proud, he presented one to his friend, Canton native (and U.S. president) William McKinley.

McKinley liked the new red flower so much that it became almost a fetish with him. He insisted on having a vaseful on his office desk at all times, and he would give the flowers out to visitors. He also took to wearing a fresh red carnation each day in his lapel. In time he came to consider it his good luck charm. He was never seen without one in his coat lapel.

On September 6, 1901, President McKinley was in Buffalo, New York, attending the Pan-American Exposition. He was scheduled to speak at the Temple of Music on the grounds of the Exposition. McKinley arrived a few minutes early and was shaking hands with some of the huge crowd who had been standing in line to enter the hall for his appearance.

A 12-year-old girl, Myrtle Ledger, of Springbrook, New York, was in line with her mother. When she suddenly found herself in front of the presi-

dent of the United States, she asked if instead of a handshake, she could have the president's red carnation. It's said that McKinley hesitated for a split second and then unpinned the flower, and smiling, handed it to little Myrtle Ledger.

Just seconds later, anarchist Leon Czolgosz approached the president with a hidden .32 caliber pistol inside a bandage wrapped around his right hand. As the president reach out to shake his hand, Czolgosz fired twice. McKinley died of his wounds eight days later.

In 1904 the Ohio legislature honored McKinley's memory by making the scarlet carnation, McKinley's good luck charm, the official state flower of Ohio.

The moral of this story is "Never give up your lucky charm."

how and exactly where started, it was probably in some suburban subdivision, the kind with the big lawns, that just screams for a riding mower. Anyone who has ever chugged up and down a big lawn on top of one of these mini-tractors knows how boring it can be. I suspect two neighbors just found a way to beat the boredom.

Though today there are hundreds of lawn mower racers across America, to my knowledge the only "lawn mower mud racers" are Ohioans—the Dewberry Mudboggers Lawnmower Racing Team. Their motto? "We just love to kick grass!"

Brutus Buckeye

COLUMBUS

Ohio State University's football mascot is a nut.

I don't mean that the person who serves as mascot is deranged. The mascot itself, Brutus Buckeye, is a nut.

In fact all of us who live in Ohio are all nuts, because we're all called "Buckeyes."

A buckeye, for those of you not familiar with it, is a large, rather useless nut that grows on a tree. Humans can't eat it and so far have found little use for it. My grandfather was of the opinion that "pigs won't even eat buckeyes." A farmer, he tried during the Great Depression to feed buckeyes to his pigs, but without success.

The name reportedly originated on September 2, 1788, at the first court of record of what was then the Northwest Territory. Colonel Ebenezer Sproat, the man who headed up the court, was greeted by Native Americans shouting what sounded like "hetuck, hetuck, hetuck," which supposedly translated as "eye of the buck." The Judge took it as a compliment. (Some humorists have claimed that the Indians were not saying "hetuck," but describing Colonel Sproat: "he-ugly.") It wasn't long before Ohioans were calling themselves "Buckeyes," too—after the native tree whose nut also looks like the "eye of a buck."

Now "Bucks" would make a lovable nickname and mascot. Why not "Ohio State Bucks"? It brings to mind a large king-of-the-forest stag that exudes pride and leadership, something to be admired. What does a nut offer?

Look at our neighbors from Michigan. They're called the "Wolverines." Now, that's a tough, crafty animal you don't want to mess with. About the only danger from a buckeye is if it should fall from the tree and hit you in the head.

At least the state symbol OSU used wasn't the state insect, the ladybug. I don't think I would like to be known as a "Ladybug." And, let's face it, our Ohio State football players might look strange running around in polka dots.

Wendy is a Buckeye

COLUMBUS

If you are a fan of Wendy's hamburgers, then you may know that Wendy herself was born here in Ohio.

The burger chain was, too. It started in 1969 in Columbus, where Dave Thomas was operating four Kentucky Fried Chicken restaurants. He did so well that he became a millionaire at the age of 35 and sold the restaurants to the parent KFC corporation.

Friends advised that there were already too many hamburger restaurants, but Thomas opened his own chain of stores anyway. He named the first one in honor of his eight-year-old daughter, Melinda. (Wendy was her nickname.) **The original Wendy's** (257 E. Broad St., Columbus; 614-464-4656) still operates. It also has a little museum exhibit where you can see the original costumes worn by Wendy's employees, as well as lots of pictures of company founder Dave Thomas and outtakes of Dave's TV commercials.

The Ghost in the Observatory

DELAWARE

The **Perkins Observatory** (Ohio Wesleyan University, 257 E. Broad St., Delaware; 740-363-1257) in Delaware has the second-largest telescope in the state of Ohio. And a ghost.

The ghost is Hiram Mills Perkins, who was a professor of mathematics and astronomy at Ohio Wesleyan from 1857 to 1907. Perkins loved the stars and was obsessed with someday building an observatory to study the cosmos. It is claimed that he wore the same suit every day for 10 years as part of his plan to save money to build an observatory. During the Civil War, he took a leave of absence to raise pigs to sell to the Union forces. The money he raised from that venture, and his frugal ways, enabled him to save up $250,000. He presented the money to the university in 1923, with the stipulation that they build an observatory of the "first magnitude." Sadly, he died before the building was completed.

Down through the years there have been reports of an old man who appears in the dome sometimes late at night and just watches as people line up to peer through the telescope. Some say it's the ghost of Hiram Perkins just checking up on his observatory.

The Big Ear
DELAWARE

Did E.T. try to call Ohio back in 1977 and we didn't answer? There's evidence that he or one of his extraterrestrial buddies did, but we didn't know how to reply.

It's gone now, but the "Big Ear" was our listening post in Ohio— for any sign of, or communication from extraterrestrial intelligence.

The Big Ear was a project of The Ohio State University and was the longest-running SETI (Search for Extra Terrestrial Intelligence) project ever conducted. It lasted from 1973 to 1998.

The "Ear" was a Kraus-type radio telescope that covered an area larger than three football fields. During its watch on the heavens it became famous for sighting some of the most distant known objects in the universe. It also received the "Wow" signal.

The "Wow" was an especially strong signal picked up in 1977 that bore all the earmarks of being extraterrestrial. It was called "Wow" because of a comment penciled in the margins of a computer printout by Jerry Ehman, one of the scientists who was working on the project. The signal was at least one lunar distance away from Earth at a time when no known satellites were near the source.

But even the demolition of Big Ear doesn't mean that we quit listening. OSU is now in the process of designing and building a next-generation radio telescope called "Argus." You can follow its progress on their website (www.bigear.org) and also get a better understanding of just how these things work.

The **Perkins Observatory** (Ohio Wesleyan University, 257 E. Broad St., Delaware; 740-363-1257) has a small exhibit about the Big Ear, as well as the original computer printout from the day the "Wow" signal was heard and a model and pictures of the Big Ear.

No, it's not your old electric-football game. This model of the "Big Ear" is all that's left of an ambitious interstellar answering machine.

More Big Ears

DUBLIN

Ohio is noted for its corn. Field corn, sweet corn—why, by late summer the state is a veritable cornucopia of ears bursting from their stalks. But Dublin is the only place in Ohio where the corn is on the stalk year round.

The Dublin Arts Council sponsored a program called "Art in Public Places," and one of the sculptures—*Field of Corn (with Osage Orange Tress)*—looks like some farmer's dreamscape. Rows and rows of human-sized corn—109 ears in all—stand upright like some kind of denuded carousel in front of a treeline of (you guessed it) Osage Orange trees. The sculpture was created by Columbus artist Malcolm Cochran in 1994. The concrete corn was cast in three different sizes to approximate the size of various humans.

The corn is supposed to celebrate Dublin's history as a farming community and to serve as a memorial to rural landscapes that have been consumed by urban development. Fittingly, it's located at Sam and **Eulalia Frantz Park** (4995 Rings Road, Dublin), a former field that belonged to a pioneer in the agriculture world who specialized in creating different kinds of corn hybrids.

This is just one of several large sculptures the Dublin Arts Council has sponsored. In **Scioto Park** (7377 Riverside Dr., Dublin) is a tribute to Leatherlips, a Wyandote Indian chief. Made of pieces of limestone, it resembles a downsized sphinx. (If you stand on top of Leatherlips's head, you have a ringside seat for whatever is playing at a nearby amphitheater.)

That's a Lot of Bull

HANOVER TOWNSHIP

If for some insane reason you feel your life won't be complete until you risk life or limb, try riding a brahma bull. You know, just like in the rodeos. The **Hang'n Tree Bull Riding Ranch** (451 Cochran Rd., Hanover Township; 513-756-9523) invites would-be cowboys to come and try riding a real bull. If you are not brave enough to ride, you can just sit in the grandstand each Friday night and watch 30 to 40 men and women see how long they can stay on the back of one of the giant bovines. The winter series bull-riding starts at the ranch every Friday at 8 p.m. It runs from mid-October through April.

Buckeye Chuck, the Weather Rodent

MARION

Yeah, yeah, I know. Punxsutawney Phil was first. The little groundhog from Pennsylvania gets lots of publicity every year, but Ohio's resident groundhog, Buckeye Chuck, is now also getting some recognition from the national media each groundhog day.

Chuck got his start many years ago when Charley Evers of Marion was working at his local radio station, WMRN. Evers's office faced a nearby woods, and over time he noted that there was a groundhog hole at the edge of the woods. He started telling folks on the radio about the antics of "Buckeye Chuck," as he named the little groundhog who lived there.

Problem was, Buckeye Chuck never came out of his hole during February. How did Evers know this? He placed a white rag on a stick and put it in the mouth of the hole so that Chuck would have to knock it over to get out.

Buckeye Chuck would usually pop out of his hole after the first few warm days in March.

Evers began to suspect that perhaps Punxsutawney Phil didn't always come out on cue either, because he checked with the state wildlife folks and they told him that groundhogs usually hibernate all winter. And if you took a sleepy groundhog out of his den in the middle of February, he darn sure wouldn't look for his shadow. He'd head right back for his hole.

But by this time the national media had heard of Buckeye Chuck as well as his rival in Pennsylvania, and started calling to see if Chuck had seen his shadow or not. Depending on Charley's mood he would assure them that the little fellow had seen his shadow and darted back into the hole, or he might say it was a cloudy day and Chuck saw nothing before running back in his den.

But then the TV reporters started arriving, expecting to see a

groundhog. Charley leveled with them and pointed to the empty hole. They would set up all day on February 2 taking pictures of Chuck's hole, waiting for him to appear. After one team harangued the town of Marion because their camera crew had wasted a whole day and hadn't seen a groundhog, Charley and his crew decided to make sure it didn't happen again.

They borrowed a groundhog from a local trapper as a stand-in for Buckeye Chuck. Evers was pretty nervous when they released the little guy from his cage because the groundhog had a rather nasty personality. "I was afraid he was going to bite someone," he admitted. The next year they tried a stuffed groundhog from the local taxidermist, to avoid the possibility of some local TV personality getting his finger bitten off.

That didn't play well either. The big-city media again started saying unkind things about Buckeye Chuck.

Then Evers had an inspiration. He contacted state wildlife officials and learned that they had this cute little woodchuck, very tame, that they used for wildlife programs in Columbus. Could Evers borrow him on February 2? Absolutely. So ever since, Buckeye Chuck arrives in Marion on February 2 in the keeping of his handler from the state wildlife division. He plods around in front of the cameras, lets reporters poke microphones and cameras at him until they have had their fill, and then he goes back to Columbus in a car to sleep the rest of the winter away.

By the way, shortly after this tradition started, Steve Stewart, then an executive with WMRN, realized what a publicity bonanza Buckeye Chuck was and, with Charley Evers, convinced a local state representative to sponsor a bill making Buckeye Chuck the state's official groundhog.

If you would like to see Buckeye Chuck, just head for Marion on February 2. Rain or shine, Chuck will be there.

Who Really Said . . .

MARION

"Ask not what your country can do for you—ask what you can do for your country." The famous quotation from John F. Kennedy's inauguration speech still reverberates through the years as a challenge to all Americans. But did he possibly borrow the quotation from another United States president?

Back on June 7, 1916, Senator Warren G. Harding of Ohio brought the Republican national convention to its feet with a real "stemwinder" of a speech. The Republicans went on to lose the presidency that year, but four years later a war-weary nation turned to the man who had made a good impression in 1916, and Harding was elected president

The Harding Home (380 Mt. Vernon Ave, Marion; 800-600-6894) still stands just as Harding left it in 1920 to go off to the White House. There, on a small monument in the rose garden, a few lines from that speech are inscribed: "We must have a citizenship less concerned about what the government can do for it . . . and more concerned about what it can do for the nation." It does have a familiar ring, though not quite as snappy as Kennedy's version.

And to be fair, Harding's own inaugural speech wasn't so captivating. (He promised a "return to normalcy.")

The Peripatetic Monument

MARION

Do you love a mystery? They have a real doozy in Marion. There is a cemetery marker that will not stay still. It's been moving for more than a hundred years.

It all started back in the 1880s when the Charles Merchant family marker was placed in the **Marion Cemetery** (630 Delaware Ave.). It was a large block of white granite, topped by an orb of solid black granite weighing more than five tons.

Two years after the ball was placed in the cemetery, workers realized that it had moved.

The unpolished base of the round granite ball was now on the side of the ball instead of underneath it. Workers got a crane and, with much effort, returned the ball to its upright position with the unpolished circle on the bottom. To insure that it did not wander again, they put a lead seal around the bottom. "That should keep the monument still for eternity," one of the workmen said.

Wrong.

Within a short time the ball began to rotate again. It's been over a century now, and the ball still moves at the rate of about an inch a month.

Hold on tight! The mysterious five-ton Merchant family marker in Marion won't sit still for anyone.

Such luminaries as radio broadcaster Paul Harvey and Robert Ripley of *Believe It Or Not* fame have investigated the roving ball, as have scientists from as far away as Russia. They have offered theories about moving mass, about heat and cold causing contractions in stone. They all sound very good, except they fail to answer one other mystery about the stone. The ball rests against the bottom stone: if it were moved, it would be scratched. But there are no scratches. It is as though a giant hand picks the stone up and gently turns it slightly. And there is a similar ball and pedestal in another part of the cemetery that has not moved even a fraction of an inch in the last century.

The moving monument has become such a tourist attraction that it is included in bus tours of the city. For more information contact the Marion Area Convention and Visitors' Bureau (1952 Marion-Mt. Gilead Road, Marion; 800-371-6688).

Napoleon's Horse
MARION

Prince Imperial, a huge white Percheron horse born in the stables of Napoleon III of France in 1865, wound up a local celebrity in Marion, Ohio.

Somehow local farmer Jacob Howser found out that the horse was for sale. He went to France, bought the animal, and imported him to the United States in 1868.

Mr. Howser believed in never cutting the horse's mane or tail, and they grew to huge lengths. He also apparently had a bit of the showman in him, since he spent a lot of time showing the horse at county and state fairs throughout the Midwest. It's reported that he would house the horse in a tent and charge a dime to see "Napoleon's Horse."

This worked pretty well and probably made Mr. Howser quite a few bucks for about 30 years. Alas, Prince Imperial eventually got old, and in 1890 he died.

Howser, businessman that he was, didn't let a little thing like death get in the way. He simply shipped the dead horse off to a taxidermist and had him stuffed, then continued to cart him from fair to fair. Come to think of it, he probably saved money. He didn't have to buy any more hay or oats.

Prince Imperial, with his long, flowing mane and tail, continued to be an attraction well into the 20th century, when he was finally retired and eventually donated to the Marion County Historical Society, and he can still be seen at **Heritage Hall** (169 East Church St., Marion; 614-387-4255).

Prince Imperial today (above) and as he appeared back in the early days of 20th century (left). I guess you just don't change much once you're stuffed.

World's Largest Collection of Popcorn Poppers and Peanut Roasters
MARION

Also at Heritage Hall is the world's largest collection of antique popcorn poppers and peanut roasters, at the **Wyandot Popcorn Museum** (169 E. Church St., Marion; 740-387-4255). Worried that your favorite model might not be included? Don't be. Museum literature assures us that "all of the classic antique poppers are here—Dunbar, Kingery, Holcome and Hoke, Stutsman, Long-Eakin, Excel, Manley, Burch, Star, Bartholomew, Olsen, and Advance"—even "the original 1890 Patent Olsen Squirrel Cage Dry Popper"(!) For those who like a little celebrity flavor, there's the 1908 Dunbar Concession Wagon used by Paul Newman to promote his gourmet popcorn.

Popcorn diehards congregate at the annual Marion Popcorn Festival in downtown Marion (which claims to be "The World's Popcorn Capital") on the Thursday, Friday, and Saturday after Labor Day.

Dixie and Other Songs
MOUNT VERNON

The song of the south was written by an Ohioan.

Daniel Decatur Emmett was born and died in Mount Vernon. He wrote a lot of music in his life, including "The Blue-tail Fly" ("Jimmy cracked corn and I don't care . . .") and "Turkey in the Straw." But he's best known for a song he wrote in 1859—"Dixie" ("I wish I was in the land of cotton . . ."). An instant hit, it was being sung in the North as well as the South when the Civil War started. But during the war, the song became the unofficial battle song of the South—much to the dismay of Emmett, who was not a Southern sympathizer.

Eventually, the song became popular again in the North, thanks to Abe Lincoln. On the night the Civil War ended, a crowd had gathered at the White House and was clamoring for a speech by the president. Lincoln came to the window, said a few words, then noticed a band in the crowd. He asked the band to play "Dixie," saying, "I've always liked the tune, and it belongs to all of us now."

Emmett is buried in **Mound View Cemetery** (307 Wooster Rd., Mt. Vernon). A memorial tribute to him donated by the Ohio division of the Daughters of the Confederacy is at the **Knox County Historical Society Museum** (875 Harcourt Rd., Mt.Vernon; 740-393-5247) A stone and plaque on South Mulbury Street mark the spot where his birthplace once stood (the house, now located off South Main Street, is open for tours by appointment with the historical society).

World's Largest Gourd Show
MT. GILEAD

The **Ohio Gourd Show** (P.O. Box 274, Mt. Gilead) bills itself as *the* place to learn about gourds.

And what might you learn about gourds? Well, they're flowering plants of the order *Cucurbitales*, for starters. The most common ones are cucumbers, watermelons, pumpkins, and squash. Some gourds are eaten; some are dried and used as containers or musical instruments. Some, apparently, just look great hanging around the house.

This show is no Johnny-come-lately; it's been held since 1962, always on the first full weekend in October. It features several buildings of gourd exhibits, gourd craft demonstrations, gourd lectures in a Gourd Theater, plenty of down-home gourd music, and . . . a hog roast.

Oh, and if you have too much hog at the roast, look for some cucurbitacin—the bitter subtance found in gourds. It's used as a purgative.

World's Biggest Basket
NEWARK

When the boss says he wants a building that looks like a basket, that's what he gets—at least at the **Longaberger Company** (One Market Square, 1500 E. Main St., Newark, 740-322-5588).

The late Dave Longaberger, when CEO of the basket firm, wanted a new corporate office building. He, company officials, and archi-

When the boss says he wants a basket-shaped world headquarters, who's going to argue? No one at the Longaberger Company.

tects met for long hours trying to decide what it should look like but were unable to agree on a plan. Dave excused himself from the meeting and left the room. A few minutes later he returned carrying the company's trademark "Market Basket."

As he set the basket on the table he said, "This is what this company is all about. This is what our office is going to look like."

Sure, there were a few obvious objections from his committee. And probably a few people who said it couldn't be done. But in the end he got what he asked for: an exact replica of the Medium Market Basket—only 160 times larger.

Today it is the centerpiece of a 25-acre corporate campus. At least 500 people work inside the seven-story building, which covers 180,000 square feet.

The basket handles, which weigh almost 150 tons, had to be set in place using giant cranes. They feature a humidity sensor that turns on heat to keep ice from forming on them. There are 84 windows in the building.

What made construction especially difficult was the basket's shape: it is smaller at the base than at the top. It is 192 feet long and 126 feet wide at ground level, but at the seventh-floor level it expands to 208 feet by 142 feet. Inside is a seven-story, 30,000-square-foot atrium. The building's offices are arranged around the atrium. There is also a 142-seat auditorium in the structure.

Visitors are welcome to stop in and look around. They do ask that large groups call ahead for a reservation.

Ohio's Hidden Park

NEWARK

Most Ohioans have never heard of it. In fact, it really doesn't exist anymore. Baughman Park is now just a collection of one man's artwork sprinkled across an overgrown woods in central Ohio.

There are statues of U.S. presidents—McKinley, Lincoln, and Washington. There are carved eagles, bas-reliefs of Native Americans, and famous generals like Ulysses S. Grant. Vandals have taken their toll: a statue of a World War I doughboy is headless, as is the statue of General William T. Sherman.

The park is even listed in the National Register of Historic Places, yet few people have seen it in recent years.

That's because of its location. It sits on a hill overlooking the giant Longaberger homestead and factory campuses where State Routes 16 and 586 come together. The property was purchased by the late basket mogul Dave Longaberger, but he didn't know quite what to do with it. Company spokesmen say they are still not sure what the future of Baughman Park will be.

Brice Baughman was a teenager when he started carving faces and things into the outcroppings of sandstone on his father's farm. Part of the farm was a quarry, and Brice learned how to cut the huge stone sections out of the earth—stone that was shipped off to build bridges and breakwalls.

It was 1902 when Brice decided to become a mortician. This left him with lots of spare time to work on his art on his farm. One after another, the statues began to accumulate, and they grew larger. He had a ready supply of sandstone.

He carved former Ohioan President Warren G. Harding. Some say he also did General George Custer who hailed from nearby New Rumley.

By the 1920s, people had heard of Baughman's forest of sculptures and were asking to see them. By the 1940s, the park was a popular spot for visitors. People would come to stare at the statues of President James Garfield and General James McPherson, or at an elephant's head, or an eagle in flight. But in 1954, when Baughman moved off the farm and into town, the park was sold. The land went through several owners, who, for the most part, left the statuary alone to take on a patina of moss and climbing weeds. The last owner had hoped to turn it into a campground, but failing health prompted the sale to the Longaberger Company that was developing the valley below. Baughman Park is not open to the public.

World's Largest Crystal Ball
WESTERVILLE

What is the world's largest crystal ball doing in a ceramics museum? It belongs there, actually, because glass is technically a ceramic.

Why make the world's largest crystal ball? Now, that's a better question, perhaps best answered by the age-old rhetorical retort, Why not? The world's largest crystal ball is, at 573 millimeters in diameter, not so big compared to other "world's largest" items, but it is pretty darn heavy—700 pounds.

The ball is just one of several notable objects on display at the **Ross C. Purdy Museum of Ceramics** (American Ceramic Society, 735 Ceramic Place, Westerville; 614-890-4700), including a missile warhead, an artificial hip joint, and a collection of presidential dinnerware. And admission is free. Aren't ceramics wonderful?

NORTHWEST

The Rice Bowl of Ohio

ARCHBOLD

You probably don't realize it, but America's favorite Asian food is made in Ohio.

La Choy Foods is located in the middle of rural Archbold, tucked away in the northwest corner of the Buckeye State.

Two friends from the University of Michigan formed the La Choy Asian Food Company in Detroit back in 1920. Wally Smith had a grocery store and wanted to offer his customers freshly grown bean sprouts. He turned to his college friend, Ilhan New, who was born in Korea, to learn how to grow them.

They started a sprout garden in Smith's bathtub. (He must have used it himself only one night a week, because the sprouts take about six days to mature.)

What brought them to Archbold? Location and handy ingredients. Northwest Ohio has lots of cows and chickens. Nearby Michigan grows a lot of celery. It's just a short drive to Pennsylvania, where they grow big mushrooms. The lake port and railroads in nearby Toledo make importation of other items pretty easy. And that's why Asian food is made in the heartland—Ohio. (Now they use large concrete vats to raise the sprouts instead of bathtubs.)

Oldest Concrete Road in America
BELLEFONTAINE

Concrete pavement usually lasts 20 to 30 years without needing major repairs, while asphalt usually holds up for only 8 to 12 years before needing resurfacing.

Think about this the next time you are sitting in a long line on an interstate highway lined with orange barrels, watching a construction crew adding new layers of asphalt to the highway. I would swear that I sometimes see the same workers year after year working on the same stretch of highway.

The city fathers of Bellefontaine must have considered these facts over a hundred years ago when they voted to pave the streets around the Logan County Courthouse. The person in charge was a man by the name of George Bartholomew, the creator of Portland concrete. What better place to demonstrate the value of concrete than the streets of his hometown? He must have done a good job. The year was 1891, and this was the first concrete highway in America; over a century later the street is still in use.

Incidentally, one of the streets around the courthouse is named McKinley Street in honor of the president, who came from Ohio. It is said to be the shortest street in the world.

Highest Point in Ohio
BELLEFONTAINE

The highest point in Ohio is not a rocky crag . . . or even much of a hill. It's a vocational school. On a gentle slope about 2 miles outside of Bellefontaine, the **Ohio Hi-Point Career Center** (2280 State Rte. 540, Bellefontaine) rises above all else in the state at an elevation of 1,549 feet. (It's closed evenings and weekends, so if you want to reach the summit of the state, go during school hours: 7 a.m. to 7 p.m, Monday through Friday.) Thanks to Campbell Hill, as the rise is known, Bellefontaine stakes its claim as "The Top of Ohio."

World's Largest Collection of Postmarks

BELLEVUE

The world's largest collection of postmark history—more than a million items—is located in two small historical buildings in Bellevue.
The museum was the dream of Margie Pfund, of Columbiana, who started collecting postmarks and postmark-related items in one room of her house in the 1940s. She started getting lots of donations and had to move the museum several times. It eventually landed in two buildings that are part of Historic Lyme Village (open in summer or by appointment; 5001 State Rte. 4, Bellevue; 419-483-4949).

Postmarks rule here, of course (the museum is run by members of the Postmark Collectors Club). They are collected here in huge numbers—mostly mounted in binders and covered with protective mylar. The museum also houses more than 1,500 publications related to postal history and a few vintage post-office boxes and cancelling stamps.

The Three Fingers of Mary Bach and Clark Gable's Pheasant

BOWLING GREEN

Three human fingers in a jar have made the Wood County Historical Center famous. I'm sure they would rather be known for the many other, normal, wonderful historical exhibits they also have on display, but it's the fingers in a jar that most schoolkids want to see when they come to visit.

The fingers belonged to Mary Bach of Bowling Green, who was savagely murdered by her husband, Carl, in October of 1881. They had not had a happy marriage, and on that day something drove Carl to get a large machete from the barn and to kill his wife, and then hack her up, cutting off bits and pieces of her body, including the three fingers, which were exhibited, pickled in a jar, during his trial.

Carl was convicted of Mary's murder, and he had the distinction of being the last man in Wood County to be hung publicly on the courthouse steps. In fact, the county sold tickets to his execution, which was held on the final day of the county fair. They really knew how to get a crowd to the county fair in those days! In fact, the tickets were in such demand that scalpers got into the act and sold tickets for much above the stated price.

The historical center also has on display the noose used in the hanging, the corn knife that Carl used to chop up his wife, and one of the tickets for admission to the hanging.

The grisly display was exhibited for many years in the Wood County courthouse, along with some other items from famous local trials, to demonstrate that crime does not pay.

When the Wood County Home was converted into a historical museum, the grim exhibit was transferred there.

The **Wood County Historical Center** (13660 County Home Rd., Bowling Green; 419-352-0967) offers a real frozen-in-time look at 19th-century rural America, from a replica of a small general store to a collection of early oil-drilling rigs. They even have a pheasant that movie star Clark Gable shot while hunting in Wood County in the 1930s.

*It's the three pickled fingers in a jar
that most schoolkids want to see
when they come to the museum.*

Remember the Maine and Pass the Soap

FINDLAY

At the close of almost every war this country gets into, patriotic citizens want a souvenir to put in their park or in front of Town Hall. Most always, these take the shape of old field guns, or sometimes a surplus tank or even an airplane (depending on the clout of the local congressional delegation).

Well, the rush was on after the 1898 Spanish-American War, when it became known that the greatest symbol of that conflict, the battleship *USS Maine*, was being raised from the floor of Havana Harbor. (It was the mysterious explosion of the *Maine* and the loss of American lives onboard that triggered the war.) Just about every community started making a pitch for a part of the old ship.

Considering that the man who had ordered the *Maine* to Cuba, President William McKinley, was an Ohioan, Ohio towns figured they'd have an edge on the competition when it came to relics.

And they did. The base of the conning tower, the command center of the *Maine*, was sent to McKinley's hometown of Canton. Other parts of the ship were made into plaques and given to Berea and Elyria.

But the real catch was made by the town of Findlay. They got the ship captain Charles Sigsbee's bathtub.

Congressman Frank Willis, from Urbana, used his influence to ask for something no one else had thought of, the captain's tub. He got it intending to donate it to his own hometown. Local folks, however, didn't see anything terribly heroic about a bathtub. They asked instead for a 10-inch shell from one of the ship's big guns.

While Urbana was saying "no thanks," the city of Boston, Massachusetts, got into the act, insisting that the tub belonged there, because that was where the ship's captain had hailed from. While the controversy swirled, the city of Findlay was heard from. They offered to take the bathtub, and because Findlay was in Congressman Willis's district, next door to Urbana, that seemed like a convenient solution. Except the navy had already delivered the bathtub to Urbana, and the mayor of Urbana was storing it in his chicken house. He refused to give it up to Findlay unless he got the 10-inch shell.

Willis finally settled the matter by talking the navy into sending the shell to Urbana, in exchange for which Urbana sent the bathtub to Findlay—allegedly C.O.D., though the town of Findlay never got around to paying.

And that was but the start of the odyssey in store for the bathtub of the *USS Maine.*

On March 3, 1913, the bathtub finally reached Findlay. Then the citizens discovered they had made a lot of fuss over a galvanized tub that had been underwater for 14 years—and it just wasn't much to

look at. Interest in the relic waned rapidly, and the tub was stored in the local municipal building. Its celebrity declined further, and the tub eventually ended up being used to store coal for the city building.

Ultimately the news broke that Findlay was using the bathtub as a coal bin, and the neighboring town of Lima jumped into the fray. They demanded the tub. But Findlay's Spanish-American War veterans came to the rescue first, hauling the tub out of the municipal building and promising to bronze it and put it in a park someplace in town. They may have had good intentions, but they wound up just putting the tub into a display case in a back hall of the Hancock County Courthouse in Findlay. It moved around the courthouse for the next 45 years, like an old soldier just fading away.

In 1960 the courthouse was renovated, and the tub was given to the Findlay College Museum. They decided the display case was more important and used that instead, putting the bathtub into storage. Then, in 1974, Findlay College was cleaning house and ended up giving the tub to the **Hancock Historical Museum** (422 W. Sandusky St., Findlay; 419-423-4433)—for *their* basement.

But the bathtub has once again been resurrected. New management at the museum has brought it out for display. It's no prettier than it was in 1913, in fact even more of the enamel is missing, and it's rusty, but it *is* a bathtub from a ship that helped start a war. And name another town that has a bathtub for a war memorial.

A Disputed Presidential Election

FREMONT

Quick. Which president of the United States was involved in a disputed election in which the vote count in Florida was crucial, and after which he had a long wait to find out if he had won?

If you answered George W. Bush, you are only half right. The first time this happened, it was to an Ohioan, Rutherford B. Hayes. In fact, his election finally had to be settled by Congress. You can learn all about this and a whole lot of other interesting things at the **Rutherford B. Hayes Presidential Center** (Spiegel Grove, Fremont; 800-998-7737). As it happens, this was also the very first presidential library and museum in the country. The former president's estate contains not only his library and museum, but also the home where he died and his grave.

Old Whitey's war record earned him a burial plot next to the President's.

Did you know that Hayes was the only Ohio president to die in Ohio? And that Lucy Webb Hayes, the president's wife, was the very first Presidential wife to be called the First Lady? That Hayes, a Civil War Veteran, was wounded four times in battle?

By the way, close to President Hayes's own grave is the final resting place of Old Whitey—the President's beloved war horse, who survived 19 battles.

The Gates of the White House in Ohio
FREMONT

They didn't pick them up at a garage sale, but it was something like that that brought the fancy ornamental iron gates that once guarded the White House in Washington, D.C., to Fremont, Ohio.

The heavy steel gates, bearing various ornamental seals, were first erected around the White House in 1871 to control horse-and-buggy traffic entering West Executive Avenue from Pennsylvania Avenue.

By the time World War I rolled around, the narrow gateways, perfect for horses and carriages, were just too small for the growing numbers of motorcars now using the streets around the White House.

In 1921 Colonel Webb C. Hayes, eldest son of former president Rutherford B. Hayes, was in Washington shopping for appropriate gates for his father's former estate in Fremont, which he had opened to the public as the country's first presidential library. Someone told Hayes about the ornamental gates around the White House, which had by now become a real traffic hazard.

Webb Hayes, who held the nation's highest award for bravery, the Medal of Honor, called on the current president, Warren G. Harding, another Ohioan, and suggested that if the White House had no further need for the gates, he would be happy to give them a good home in Ohio. Harding was delighted with the idea, but when congressmen heard about the deal they said, "Wait a minute." The gates belonged to the country, and it was up to Congress to decide how they were to be disposed of.

Despite Harding's backing, it took Hayes six years of persistence and legal wrangling with bureaucrats and Congress to finally have the gates, which were no longer in use, transferred to the Fremont estate.

The ornamental gates that guarded the White House during the stay of every president from Ulysses Grant to Calvin Coolidge, can now be seen at the six entrances to the **Rutherford B. Hayes Presidential Center** (Spiegel Grove, Fremont; 800-998-7737) thanks to the persistence of Colonel Webb C. Hayes, who refused to take "no" for an answer.

The Historic Privy of Genoa

GENOA

Picture this. It's the nation's bicentennial, and your little community is feeling a bit left out. Towns and villages all over America are sprucing up old buildings and putting them on the National Register of Historic Places to do their part for America's big birthday celebration.

But the oldest building you've got is . . . a bit unusual.

That's what happened in Genoa. Their oldest building, which had been built around the

GENOA
Inc. 1868
SITE OF HISTORIC
TOWN HALL
and
"LITTLE BUILDING"
(Old School Privy)

time of the Civil War, was a small brick structure out behind a local school. It definitely showed its age, but contractors said that with some repairs—expensive repairs—it would probably look as good as new.

The problem was, their building had originally served the teachers and the students of the local school as their "little house." The building was a 12-hole brick privy.

Genoa keeps current, of course, and the school had long ago stopped using the privy for its original purpose. It had survived, probably, because of its size, and the fact that it was, well, built like a brick privy! So the holes had been filled in and the seats taken out, and it became a storage building for the school janitor. Down through the years, many people had even forgotten what the little building's original purpose was.

But locals weren't shy when it came to saving their decrepit old toilet building, and they convinced their congressman that the building was indeed worth renovating. He managed to get a grant through Congress, and once the paperwork was done, Genoa, Ohio, became the only community in America with an outhouse listed on the National Register of Historic Places.

Hard to Swallow

LIMA

Estey Yingling started the collection. His son, Walter "Bud" Yingling, continued it and ultimately donated it to the **Allen County
Museum** (620 W. Market St., Lima; 419-222-9426). Father and son, both physicians (ear, nose, and throat specialists), collected objects swallowed
by local residents (including patients at nearby Lima Mental Hospital). "I've never actually counted them," said John Carnes, curator of
this, the largest county museum in Ohio, "but there's well over a hundred." Asked what might be the prize of the collection, Carnes said,
"There's a very large wood screw that kind of stands out."

The museum collection also boasts a John Dillinger exhibit (he
broke out of the local jail in 1933 and killed a sheriff), a restored
Sherman tank, a large collection of albino animals (stuffed), and a
children's museum.

OBJECTS REMOVED FROM ESOPHAGUS, BRONCHIAL TREE (LUNGS), AND LARYNX OF PATIENTS OF DRS. ESTEY C. YINGLING AND WALTER E. YINGLING.

HANG OUT WITH FAMOUS (DEAD) FOLKS

Do you want to hang out with famous people? Try visiting any one of dozens of Ohio cemeteries. Lots of famous people called Ohio home at one time, or had a special attraction to the Buckeye State—so much so that they decided to spend eternity here.

For example, at the Greenlawn Cemetery in Columbus, you can hobnob with Samuel Prescott Bush. He is the paternal grandfather of former president George Bush, and great-grandfather of President George W. Bush. He's in section 56, southwest of the chapel.

Not far away in that same cemetery you'll find Captain Eddie Rickenbacker, the World War I hero known as the "Ace of Aces" for the number of German planes he shot down. He later founded Eastern Airlines, which is now just a memory in aviation history.

Rickenbacker is just around the corner from Roy Stanislaus. Who was he? Stanislaus was a sergeant in the cavalry on the day Custer was wiped out at Little Big Horn. Stanislaus won the Medal of Honor for bringing water to the wounded during the famous battle.

In Spring Grove Cemetery in Cincinnati, you can visit Salmon P. Chase, secretary of the treasury during the Lincoln administration and member of the Supreme Court. And Powell Crosley, Jr., who invented the refrigerator bearing his name. (He also invented a tiny car called the Crosley and owned the Cincinnati Reds.) Also buried here is Charles Fleischman, the yeast manufacturer, James Norris Gamble (as in Procter & ...); William Cooper Procter (the other half); Jesse and Hannah Grant, parents of president Ulysses Grant; famed New York Yankees manager

Miller Huggins; Bernard Kroger, who started the Kroger Grocery Store empire; several members of the McCook family (see "The Fighting McCooks"); and Alexander McGuffey of McGuffey Readers.

In Cleveland's Lake View Cemetery, you'll find songwriter and singer Ernest Roland Ball (see "When Irish Eyes are Smiling") and Helene Hathaway Britton, who once owned the St. Louis Cardinals (the first woman to own a major league baseball club). There is a mass grave here honoring the 172 students and two teachers who died in America's biggest school fire, the Collinwood School Fire, on March 4, 1908. Former Ohio governor Harry Davis is also buried here, as well as James Garfield, the assassinated 20th U.S. president. (Technically, he and his wife, Lucretia Garfield, are not really buried here. Their bodies rest in a crypt beneath the monument that dominates this cemetery.) Also in Lake View Cemetery you'll find Coburn Haskell, the inventor of the modern golf ball; John Hay, private secretary to Abraham Lincoln and secretary of state to William McKinley; Dayton Clarence Miller, who produced the first X-ray of the human body; Gloria Pressman, one of the original "little rascals" of the movies; and the world's richest man, John D. Rockefeller, Sr. Have you ever tasted Salisbury steak? It was created by Dr. James Salisbury, who is also buried in Lake View Cemetery. Also buried here is Carl Stokes, the first African-American to be elected mayor of a major U.S. City.

Down in Dayton at Woodland Cemetery, there is a gathering of equally famous people, including Paul Laurence Dunbar, the first black poet to win renown in the United States and a friend of the Wright brothers, the guys who built the first airplane. The Wright brothers are also buried here, as is Charles Kettering, the man who prevented countless broken arms by inventing the self-starter for cars. Test pilot Frank Patterson rests here; it was a plane crash that took his life. His name lives on as the "Patterson" of Wright-Patterson Air Force Base. There is another Patterson buried here, and he is responsible for cash registers all over the world. John Patterson founded the National Cash Register Corporation.

In the nearby Miami Valley Memory Gardens at 1639 E. Lytle-Five Points Road in Dayton, you will find the grave of a man who had a profound effect on the world—Ermal C. "Ernie" Fraze. He was the inventor of the "pull tab" that opens countless cans of beer and soft drinks.

Mystery Hill

MARBLEHEAD

"Visit Mystery Hill and defy the laws of nature and gravity," the sign says. Well, that's hard to resist. And besides, it comes complete with dinosaurs. **Mystery Hill** (8232 E. Harbor Rd., Marblehead; 419-798-5230) fits right in here in Ohio's "vacationland."

Our guide, who appeared to be 10 or 11 years old, warned us that "horses have been known to stampede and small children become hysterical" upon seeing what we were about to experience.

Inside the rather tumble-down building, our "guide" put a golf ball in a trough and it ran uphill. He then pumped a pump, and the water ran uphill. Sensing he was not impressing his audience, the lad cheerfully announced, that he would overcome gravity in a "death-defying act," and with that he placed the back legs of a kitchen chair on a two-by-four nailed to the wall, hopped on the seat, and seemingly hung in space supported only by the two back legs.

The tilted floor made all of us feel as though we were walking at a 45° tilt.

Our young guide informed us that the hillside location was chosen for this attraction because of its "massive gravitational pull from the center of the earth."

You can't miss Mystery Hill's sister attraction, Prehistoric Forest—a 15-foot-tall fiberglass dinosaur stands guard in front of a fake mountain that belches fluorescent colored flames and features a manmade waterfall. That'll get you in the mood for a stroll through the forest.

There are 19 life-size beasts, including a triceratops and a T-Rex. Some are displayed in wooded glades, others in marshy ponds. A couple of them make some noise and have mechanical heads that wig and wag, but if you're looking for "animatronic" dinosaurs this is not the place to find them. Here they pretty much just stand and stare at you. All in all, even the smallest child will probably not be frightened by an afternoon walk through here.

"Horses have been known to stampede and small children become hysterical," warned our young guide.

The Marblehead Muffler Man

MARBLEHEAD

"Muffler Man" is a designation given to huge fiberglass statues of men or women, usually cradling a product in their arms, often along major highways, and near especially publicity-minded businesses. Originally some of them were used to promote muffler shops, hence the name. One such Muffler Man has stood on the Marblehead Peninsula for over a quarter of a century, but most folks can't remember what he was selling or how he got there. He stands, 20 feet tall but empty handed now, in front of a camper-trailer business. Most locals say it's been years since they have seen "Big Pierre," as they call him, sell anything. Standing guard along State Route 163, Pierre laughs at the rain and the snow. In fact nothing seems to bother him except the passing of time.

But Big Pierre is really Big Jacques. He started life in Mansfield as the representative of Jacques Roast Beef Sandwiches. His arms, which once reportedly held a sandwich or a pizza box, are just skeletal frames now. His white sailor hat is dirty and disfigured. His present owner, Young's Travel Trailers, says he is for sale.

A Very Happy Walleye to You
PORT CLINTON

On New Year's Eve in Times Square, a crystal glass apple is lowered down a tower to announce the transition from one year to the next. That's because New York is popularly known as the Big Apple.

Well, little Port Clinton, Ohio, decided to get in on the act. And what would you expect to find in the port whose 1,000 chartered fishermen take in about 70 percent of Lake Erie's walleye catch each year? That's right: a 20-foot-long fiberglass walleye named Captain Wylie.

Can it be long until the New Year's Eve when TV cameras will switch instead to the frosty shores of Lake Erie to watch Captain Wylie drop in Port Clinton?

Captain Wylie, a 20-foot-long walleye, appears ready to swallow a 4-foot-tall child.

Big Fruit

PORT CLINTON

Of course, if Port Clinton wants to compete with the Big Apple, they can also compete with their . . . big apple. A five-foot-tall Red Delicious stands out along the roadside at **Bergman's Fruit Farm** (Catawba Rd., just north of the U.S. Rte. 2 interchange).

The Ship on the Island

PUT-IN-BAY

On the ferry ride back from South Bass Island to Port Clinton, a lot of people grab for the camera and a few stare in disbelief upon seeing a Great Lakes ore boat stuck into a cliff, hundreds of feet above the water. It looks for all the world as if a giant storm had deposited the ship, bow forward, on this cliff overlooking the lake.

Don't bother to look through the tourist books for it. There are no brochures, no maps pointing it out, and no explanations of how it got there.

The story behind the ship is becoming a Lake Erie legend, though.

The ship began life nearly 80 years ago as the *Benson Ford* flagship of the Ford Motor Company's fleet of lake freighters. Henry Ford named it after one of his grandsons. He took a special interest in the ship and had luxury accommodations put into its forward section—walnut-paneled staterooms, a fireplace in a gathering room, a special kitchen, special plumbing. It was a ship that was to be fit for a king, or at least the founder of an auto dynasty. Whether Henry Ford ever actually sailed on the *Benson Ford* is a matter of conjecture, but certainly many of the top Ford executives and their families made use of the luxury quarters over the half-century that it sailed the Great Lakes. It was retired from service and scheduled to be cut up for scrap in 1986.

At that time, Frank and Lydia Sullivan were looking for a summer home on the Lake Erie Islands. Finding nothing they liked, they were considering building one when Frank heard that the *Benson Ford* was being scrapped. Discovering that the owner's quarters had been constructed for Henry Ford, he realized that it would be very special. That's when a dream was born: to cut off the front of the *Benson Ford*, from the owner's quarters all the way up to the pilothouse, and move it to South Bass Island for a home.

After thousands and thousands of dollars, and hours and hours of frustration, finally the front section was cut away and loaded onto a huge barge that then towed the *Benson Ford* (now renamed, of course, the *Frank Sullivan*) 60 miles west from Cleveland to the Lake Erie Islands.

Frank and Lydia purchased a landlocked lot on a small hill overlooking the water on the western edge of South Bass Island. Both sea-borne and land-based cranes made the final transfer of the *Frank Sullivan* from the barge onto a solid bedrock foundation, the bow nearly hanging over the 18-foot cliff above the water. And the *Benson Ford/Frank Sullivan* was home from the seas.

After spending thousands of more dollars in heat, electrical, and plumbing hookups, the Sullivans were ready to tackle the renovation of the quarters in their boat home.

Over the next 13 years, the *Frank Sullivan* was the summer home they had planned. At one point they even considered turning the landmark into a bed and breakfast to help offset some of the enormous costs they had incurred moving the ship to the islands. However, because their lot was landlocked, their neighbors were required by law only to allow the Sullivans access to their home, not to tolerate commercial traffic.

That effectively stopped any commercial use of the unusual home. And when the Sullivans decided to finally sell the ship home in 1999, there was a new problem. How do you price something unique? There was nothing even remotely similar to it anywhere. So they finally put the place up for public auction. They advertised it for weeks and drew inquiries from 10 states and Canada. The big day finally arrived on September 21, 1999. The ship residence was sold for $451,000 to two local automobile dealers. There had been speculation that the unusual residence would bring as much as a million or more dollars.

The *Frank Sullivan* can be seen by arriving and departing ferryboat passengers on the west side of South Bass Island. It is still a private home and is not open to the public.

The Longest Bar in the World
PUT-IN-BAY

If it pleases you to see a bartender sling a couple of cold brews down a wet bar, you have to see the bar at the **Beer Barrel Saloon** (324 Delaware St., Put-in-Bay; 419-285-2337) on South Bass Island in Lake Erie.

Their bar is the longest in the world, according to the *Guinness Book of World Records*. To put it in perspective, if you stood the bar on end it would be taller than the island's other main tourist attraction, the Perry Peace Memorial monument. It's 405 feet, 10 inches long. It has 160 bar stools, and 56 beer taps, and on a busy night more than 20 bartenders work behind it.

Rudolph the Ohio Reindeer

RUDOLPH

Rudolph, Ohio, is little more than a wide spot in the highway in northwest Ohio. The population in and around the little town is probably less than a thousand. But when the Christmas season arrives, hundreds of thousands of letters pour into the little town's post office.

Marsha Deitemyer is the officer in charge of the **Rudolph post office** (Rudolph Postmaster, P.O. Box 9998, Rudolph, Ohio 43462). She says last Christmas she and her husband and two kids worked almost every night to hand-cancel more than 130,000 pieces of mail that had been sent to Rudolph to be remailed with the Rudolph postmark.

The postmark is applied with a rubber stamp marked "Reindeer Station," with a small picture of the reindeer with a glowing nose.

Marsha says the mail comes from all over America, and that the post office has been providing the holiday service for several years.

Don't forget, if you send your boxed cards to Marsha to remail and cancel, you have to have proper postage on each envelope. It's the holidays and Marsha has the holiday spirit, but she's not going to pay for your postage.

A Place Where They Write on Your Buns

TOLEDO

Tony Packo's would probably be just another neighborhood bar in Toledo had it not been for some very famous customers. One was a skinny kid who grew up nearby and went on to become a TV star. Jamie Farr played Corporal Max Klinger on the hit TV show *M*A*S*H*, and in many of the shows he made mention of his longing for a Hungarian hot dog from Tony Packo's. The real-life Tony Packo's benefited greatly from the national and worldwide exposure. Jamie Farr, they say, has free hot dogs at Tony Packo's for life.

But an earlier brush with fame, in 1972, also had an impact on the business. Movie star Burt Reynolds was performing in *The Rainmaker* at a Toledo-area theater, and Nancy Packo, Tony's daughter, wrote him a note and suggested that since he had to eat somewhere, he should try their place.

Two nights later, much to everyone's surprise, Reynolds and other cast members walked in. The Packo family wanted Reynolds to sign his autograph to something that they could put on the wall. They searched for a blank piece of paper, but none could readily be found, so in their haste to mark the night, someone grabbed a stale hot-dog bun and offered that to Reynolds to sign.

Now, local and national celebrities get asked to sign the darnedest things—everything from ladies' underwear to a bare chest. So the fact he was signing his autograph on a hot-dog bun probably didn't even phase Reynolds. But in that moment a tradition was born.

Today there are more than a thousand autographed hot-dog buns mounted throughout the restaurant. They bear the

Nice buns, Leslie Uggams.
You too, Mel Tormé!

THE ONLY STATE WITHOUT A FLAG

Ohio is the only state without a flag. Ohio's "flag" is, technically, not a flag but a burgee. A burgee is a sort of twin-tailed pennant. Ohio is the only state that uses one.

It was designed by John Eisemann, a state official. The large blue triangle represents Ohio's hills and valleys, while the white and red stripes are said to represent roads and waterways. The stars, 13 of them, in the blue field represent the original 13 colonies of the United States. Four stars at the peak of the blue field are for the states added after the initial 13 and point to Ohio as the 17th state admitted to the Union. It is claimed that the large red circle surrounded by a white "O" stands for "Ohio."

Historian Richard McElroy points out that the burgee was first flown at the Ohio building at the Pan-American Exposition in 1901 and closely resembles a banner carried by explorer Christopher Columbus on his expedition to the New World in 1492. Since our state capital was named for Columbus, it's possible that the explorer also influenced the design of the Ohio flag, which was adopted by the legislature in 1902.

signatures of five U.S. presidents, as well as first ladies, sports figures, local celebrities (like traveling reporters!), and, of course, Burt Reynolds, the man who started it all.

Tony Packo II, who took over the restaurant from his father, says to his knowledge it's the only collection of autographed hot-dog buns in the world.

But here's a secret: they aren't real. Tony says that the very first ones were, but they started to turn green and disintegrate pretty quickly, so they sent a mold of a bun to a factory and had some styrofoam buns made. Unless you bite into one, you can't tell the difference.

The Packos now operate a chain of restaurants in northwest Ohio, but the original **Tony Packo's** (1902 Front Street, Toledo; 419-691-6054), where Corporal Klinger first enjoyed a Hungarian hot dog, is still at the same location.

Neptune, the Real Navy SEAL

TOLEDO

Toledo is home to a real U.S. Navy SEAL—a seal that joined the U.S. navy. His name is Neptune, and to be honest he probably never wanted to join our navy; he was shanghaied into it back in 1974, when he was just a pup. He was netted by the navy near his birthplace in Iceland, then whisked to the American west coast, where he became part of a contingent of marine mammals that were going to be trained for military defense.

It was all part of an experiment that grew out of the navy's discovery that dolphins could be trained to work with humans. They thought the same might be done with seals.

The seals did learn to retrieve missing training mines, and they could also be taught to turn large valves using their flippers. They could dive to great depths without the need to decompress as humans do.

But after four years, Neptune's hitch was up when he became blind. What do you do with a Navy SEAL veteran when he really *is* a seal, and is now disabled?

Neptune was first retired to Mystic Aquarium in Connecticut and later transferred to the Indianapolis Zoo. But when the **Toledo Zoo** (U.S. Rte. 25, Toledo; 419-385-5721) installed its new state-of-the-art Arctic Encounter, with a 210,000-gallon saltwater pool, Neptune had a permanent home.

Today, at 700 pounds, he devours 22 pounds of fish each day and has two younger female seals in the tank to keep him company. He seems to be enjoying his retirement as he entertains thousands of visitors each year.

The Ohio-Michigan War

TOLEDO

Ohio and Michigan have been battling for decades on the gridiron. It's one of the great rivalries of college football. But did you know that the two states once nearly declared war on each other?

Accounts of the Ohio-Michigan war read almost like the plot of a

Three Stooges movie. They involve a 19-year-old "boy governor," both states' militias, and the "Great Swamp" that used to cover most of northwest Ohio. It might have been a real shooting war, but the two militias got lost in the swamp and wandered around for a week trying, without success, to find each other. Here's how it happened.

Toledo, Ohio, was once known as Toledo, Michigan. In 1835, the tiny village that would one day grow into a city anchoring the western end of Lake Erie was considered to be part of the land owned by Michigan. In that year, Michigan had petitioned Congress for statehood. According to the Northwest Ordinance, its southern boundary should have been drawn from the tip of Lake Michigan eastward to Lake Erie, which would put the mouth of the Maumee River, and what was to become Toledo, in Michigan.

Ohio, which had been a state since 1803 and had a larger population, realized that whoever controlled the mouth of the Maumee also controlled shipping. So Ohioans started pressuring Congress to move the line to North Cape, giving control of Maumee Bay to Ohio.

Now, for some reason President Andrew Jackson had appointed 19-year-old Stevens T. Mason as the governor of Michigan Territory, and the young man proved to be a stormy leader. He fired off a warning to Ohio that he would not hesitate "to resist to the utmost every encroachment or invasion upon the rights and soil of this territory."

Rather than back off, Ohio governor Robert Lucas showed up in Perrysburg, Ohio, along with 300 Ohio militiamen.

Michigan's boy governor wasn't to be frightened. He called out a posse of sheriff's deputies, who were in reality members of the Michigan militia, and they marched to Monroe and what seemed a certain shooting war with the Ohioans.

Local folks took it seriously. Settlers filled their wagons with families and took off. Men were galloping in and out of the two towns with guns at the ready. They finally moved toward each other.

Today, the trip between Toledo and Monroe, Michigan, is about a 20-minute drive up I-75. But this was 1835, and the region was a heavily wooded swamp. Both militia forces wandered through the bogs and woods day after day without seeing any of the "enemy." Truth is, they were probably lost, and both sides eventually gave up and went back home after a week in the wilderness.

Both militias wandered through the bogs and woods without seeing any of the "enemy." After a week, they gave up and went back home.

President Jackson was known to support Ohio for political reasons and so was mistrusted by his Michigan appointee, Governor Mason. So when Jackson asked Mason to allow Ohio commissioners to run a survey of the disputed boundary line to just north of Point Place, Mason refused.

Finally Ohio governor Lucas sent his surveyors out on April 26, but they were met by a posse of sheriff's deputies, who ordered them to leave. When the Ohioans refused, shots were fired.

Perhaps they were all just lousy shots, but no one was hit in the exchange. The sheriff did arrest the Ohioans and charge them with violating the Pains and Penalties Act, which prohibited Ohioans from exercising any authority in Michigan.

The only bloodletting during the whole Ohio-Michigan War occurred when Michigan militia general Jacob Brown, of Tecumseh, started rounding up any Ohioans he found on Michigan territory. This included the entire family of Ohio major Benjamin Franklin Stickney. The major was tied to his horse for the trip to the Monroe jail. The major had two sons. Not being very imaginative, he had named one of them One and the other Two. Well, Two didn't like seeing his father hauled off to jail, and at the jail he grabbed a knife and swung it at Monroe County sheriff Joseph Wood, slashing him in the thigh, and making the sheriff the only casualty of the "war."

The whole matter was finally settled when Congress allowed Michigan to become a state if it agreed to give up the Toledo area and accepted the western end of the Upper Peninsula in exchange for the Maumee harbor.

At least they thought it was settled. As late as 1972, the U.S. Supreme Court listened to arguments from attorneys that Toledo actually belonged in Michigan. But this time the governors didn't call out the militia. By the way, Toledo is still in Ohio.

NORTHEAST

A Hotel with Round Rooms

AKRON

You'll never be "cornered" in a round room. You can make that observation when you stay at **The Crowne Plaza Akron at Quaker Square** (135 S. Broadway, Akron; 330-253-5970).

The rooms really are round. And almost totally soundproof. They were carved out of a cluster of 36 concrete silos once used by the Quaker Oats Company to store the grain that they used to make such things as Quaker Oats. (Remember "The cereal shot from guns"?) When the complex, which had been built around the turn of the 20th century, was finally abandoned when the parent company moved to Chicago, the city fathers in Akron started looking around for a new use for the site, which is very near downtown Akron.

The answer was an innovative idea to turn the old mill into a shopping center and the silos into a hotel. Work started in 1973, and the hotel opened about two years later.

The silos, listed on the National Register of Historic Places, are each 120 feet tall and 24 feet in diameter. The hotel can claim to be the only hotel in the world where all the rooms are round.

The Akron Airdock

AKRON

It sits at the edge of an airfield. In the twilight you might think it was the body of some giant prehistoric animal, all dark grays and black, merging with the night.

The Airdock in Akron was built in 1929 by the Goodyear Tire & Rubber Company to construct and house giant rigid airships, which were three or four times longer than today's blimps.

How big is it? It's equal in height to a 22-story building, and you could play seven football games side by side on the floor inside. It is twice the length of the Washington Monument. When it was built, it boasted the largest continuous area ever contained under one roof.

Each of the spherical doors weighs 600 tons and is fastened at the top with a steel pin 17 inches in diameter and six feet long.

This is a place of legend. The hollow building has been known to develop its own weather. Clouds form, and light rain has even fallen inside. Outside, after a heavy snow, they once experienced an avalanche of snow off the rounded roof that was so heavy a nearby security office at the base of the building was flattened.

No tours are allowed in the building, but the exterior of the Air-dock can be seen from just about anywhere near the airport or from Kelley Avenue, near the Carousel Dinner Theater.

Largest Sandstone Quarry in the World
AMHERST

Amherst Township has a mighty big hole.

It also has a large sign over its bandstand proclaiming "Amherst, Ohio, Sandstone Center of the World." The two items go together, of course; many homes and businesses are made partly or entirely from sandstone that came from the giant quarries just outside of town.

American Stone Cleveland Quarries (8705 Quarry Rd., Amherst; 800-248-0250) has been quarrying and fabricating sandstone here since 1868. The quarries cover a thousand acres and contain over 300 million cubic feet of stone. The quarry hole in Amherst known as Buckeye Number One is believed to be the largest sandstone quarry hole in the world. It can easily be seen from Quarry Road, which runs from South Amherst to Amherst. Sandstone from here was used to build the John Hancock Building in Boston, the Hockey Hall of Fame in Toronto, and Buffalo's city hall.

The Headless Chicken

ASHTABULA

A little over a half-century ago, a chicken in Ashtabula, entered the record books and probably caused more than a few nightmares.

On New Year's Eve, 1946, John and Helen Marrison were preparing to celebrate with a nice chicken dinner. Back in those days, at least in Ashtabula, when you wanted chicken for dinner you didn't head for the freezer. You picked up your ax and headed to the chicken coop. John did just that, selecting an especially active White Rock rooster that had probably awakened him too early one too many times. As he had done countless times before, John grabbed the rooster by the legs and laid its neck against an old railroad tie.

Knowing that his wife was rather partial to cooked chicken necks (she considered them a delicacy), John aimed high with his impromptu guillotine. He had grown up on a farm and had dispatched hundreds of chickens, and there didn't seem to be anything unusual about this job; the head parted from the body as expected, and the bird flopped around a bit and then went still.

John was now overdue for work at the gasoline station, so he pushed the lifeless bird into a bucket and carried it down to his basement, leaving the messy plucking job to his wife.

But when Helen Marrison later went to prepare the bird, the bucket was empty. Then she saw it—a headless chicken running in circles around her basement!

For some people an incident like this would be nightmarish, but Helen Marrison was made of sterner stuff. She just picked up the phone and called her husband. John assured her this was probably just a delayed muscle reaction and that the bird would soon lie down permanently, and she would then be able to get it ready for the cooking pot.

But when John came home that evening and went into the basement, there was the rooster still walking around!

The sight of the headless rooster, alive and kicking, kind of dulled John and Helen's appetite for fresh chicken. So they then decided to try and help the rooster continue his battle to live. John put some spider webs into the still-seeping wound where the head used to be to help stop the bleeding, and he placed the bird in a box.

Over the next few days, neighbors heard about the strange event and began tramping through John and Helen's house to see the headless wonder. Then the media caught on. The local paper, the *Ashtabula Star Beacon*, ran a front-page story on January 2 reporting that the rooster was "as perky as can be" and "strutting around the living room." The rush was on. Reporters from Cleveland and even national papers started to descend on Ashtabula, stopping at the police station for directions to the home of the headless walking chicken.

That was when Mrs. L. B. Butler of the Ashtabula Humane Society got into the act. Mrs. Butler arrived at the Marrison home with two sheriff's deputies in tow, demanding that John immediately dispose of the rooster in a humane manner.

John refused. He reasoned the rooster really wanted to live and didn't seem to be in any pain, and in fact was acting almost normal. Instead of dispatching the bird, he took it to Doctor Whitwood, a Jefferson veterinarian. The doctor performed some minor surgery on the bird's neck so that more food and water could be fed directly into its crop, along with a little gravel to help digestion. When he came out of the operating room, he said it was his opinion that because the brain—located in the head—is what tells us if we are in pain, the rooster must not be feeling any ill effects.

The Humane Society backed off and left the matter to be argued in the newspapers over the next few weeks. Some readers urged the bird be saved; others argued that the rooster must be hurting and should be put to sleep.

While all this was going on, John Marrison said the rooster seemed content. He fed it every day, using a spring from an old corset and an apple peeler to force the food into the bird's digestive system.

But then in February, while feeding the bird, John accidentally disturbed the scab over the place where the head used to be, and despite John's continued efforts, the bird began to weaken. It died, for real this time, a day later, on February 7, 1947.

By now John had really grown attached to the bird, so he sent it to a taxidermist to be mounted. He kept it for many years in his garage. John was never again able to kill a chicken. But he did admit that he sometimes would order chicken in a restaurant.

Covered Bridges
AUSTINBURG

The folks in Ashtabula County believe that old-fashioned wooden bridges still have a place when it comes to crossing creeks and rivers. The County Engineer's Office has been repairing old covered bridges—and even building *new* covered bridges.

Ashtabula County currently has 16 covered bridges within its borders—four of them built since 1983, when officials first decided to build a wooden covered bridge to replace another bridge on State Road in Monroe Township.

But that's not all. County officials are now finishing plans for the longest covered bridge in America. The new bridge will span the Ashtabula River on State Road. It may hang suspended 90 feet over the river, and should be completed in 2003.

The Ashtabula County Convention and Visitor's Bureau (1850 Austinburg Rd., Austinburg, 800-337-6746) has a map showing the bridges.

The Big Easy of Austinburg
AUSTINBURG

Remember the song "Ol' rockin' chair's got me. . ."?

Rocking chairs seem to have a special place in the hearts of Americans, from the time we are rocked in one as a baby until the sunset of our lives, when we rock away the time that is left to us. But perhaps no rocking chair is as special as this one alongside the highway in Austinburg.

The chair, which stands about 25 feet high, is currently an advertisement for a furniture company that owns the site, but over the years it has been owned by several other firms, including a lumberyard and a video store.

The present owner told me the chair had been built sometime in the 1960s or '70s, and a previous owner had assured him that the chair was listed in a book of records somewhere as the "World's Biggest Boston Rocking Chair."

Maybe it is. At least I couldn't find any listings for bigger giant Boston rocking chairs. If you're out Austinburg way, judge for yourself. The chair is located on the west side of State Route 45, at the north end of the village of Austinburg.

Behalt

BERLIN

Heinz Gaugel had a dream. A rather big dream. He was an artist, and the masterpiece he dreamed of turned out to be a painting 10 feet tall and 265 feet long.

Gaugel, a German soldier in World War II and former prisoner of war held by the Americans, was rebuilding his life in his new country, Canada. He was a self-taught painter, and his work was starting to draw attention, especially his large murals.

While traveling in the early 1960s, Gaugel happened to stop in Berlin, Ohio. At the time he was unaware of the Amish and Mennonite people, but he did recognize the fact that these plainly dressed folk spoke German.

Heinz was so captivated by the Amish and their ways that he decided to stay and tell their story in a huge painting.

This was no easy matter. The Amish, as part of their religion, shun photos and likenesses of themselves. According to Paul Miller of the Mennonite Information Center, the Amish have seen their beliefs twisted and used for personal gain by others who came to the farming community and wanted to exploit them, so Heinz at first got very little help or encouragement from them.

However, he delved into the history books and did such a good research job that by the time he started to paint his mural, he had impressed many of the locals with his sincerity.

To some he was "that crazy German" who worked to the sound of Beethoven in an old one-room schoolhouse at the corner of U.S. Route 62 and Mt. Hope Road. He had a canvas stretched all the way around the room. Books were everywhere, and standing on the floor he would use a long stick with a charcoal pencil at the end to sketch in the figures that he would later paint.

He worked for 20 years on the painting. It was completed in 1992. He called it *Behalt*, which means "to hold" or "to remember."

The giant circular painting is mounted in a specially built circular room at the **Amish and Mennonite Heritage Center** (County Rd. 77, Berlin; 330-893-3192). It is considered one of only a half-dozen cycloramic paintings in the world and one of the biggest. What is more incredible is that Gaugel did it all by himself. He hired no other painters to help. It was almost an obsession in the last third of his life. And the most wonderful thing is that his work is appreciated by the Amish and the Mennonites. It is not unusual to see groups of Amish children being led around the room, gazing at a painted mural of their history.

Gaugel later painted a series of regular-sized paintings that portrayed American folk heroes like Johnny Appleseed, and he did several religious works. He was working on one when he died on December 28, 2000, at the age of 73.

"That crazy German" spent 14 years creating one of the world's largest cycloramic paintings in tiny Berlin, Ohio.

World's Largest Amish Buggy
BERLIN

What do you do if you are opening a new business in the heart of the world's largest Amish community and you want to get the attention of the tourists?

Obviously, you build a giant buggy.

That, at least, is what the owners of **Wendell August Forge** (U.S. Rte. 62, Berlin; 330-893-3713) did.

Their buggy sits in the middle of a barn-like showroom. Its front wheels alone are 5 feet high; the entire buggy is 7 feet, 4 inches wide and 10 1/2 feet high. The driver's seat is up about as high as the seat in a tractor-trailer rig. It would take a horse about twice the size of a Clydesdale to pull the vehicle.

Fort Laurens and Ohio's Unknown Soldier
BOLIVAR

It's a little-known fact that Ohio had a small part in the Revolutionary War. In what was then wilderness frontier, Fort Laurens was built in 1778 and named in honor of Henry Laurens, then president of the Continental Congress.

It was an ill-conceived plan to build a fort so far from the Continental Army's supply lines. The idea was to wage a campaign to attack the British at Detroit. But between the banks of the Tuscarawas River at Bolivar, where Fort Laurens was located, and Detroit were hundreds of fierce Native Americans loyal to the British.

The British and the Indians easily cut the supply lines and surrounded the fort.

The starving garrison was surrounded and under siege for more than a month before being forced to abandon the fort in 1779.

Today there is just a faint outline where the fort once stood. The Ohio Historical Society maintains the **Fort Laurens State Memorial** (open Apr.–Oct., Fort Laurens Rd., Bolivar; 800-283-8914) on part of the land where the fort was. Remains of the soldiers who died defending the fort are buried in a crypt in the museum. Except for one.

In the 1970s, while repairs to a parking lot at the museum were being done, another body was found—the body of an American officer who had died fighting at Fort Laurens. It was decided that he would become Ohio's own "unknown soldier," and he was buried with full military honors in an above-ground crypt in the middle of the park. The inscription on his grave reads, "Tomb of the Unknown Patriot of the American Revolution."

There's only one problem. Later research uncovered his identity, and researchers now say they know who's buried in the tomb of the "Unknown Patriot." (So far, though, there are no plans to make any changes to the tomb.)

Howl with the Wolves

BOLIVAR

A wolf was last seen running wild in Ohio back around 1850. After that, most of them headed for less populous states.

But Marty Huth has always had a fascination with wolves, so he applied to the U.S. Fish and Wildlife Service and obtained a permit to raise his own pack of wolves for an educational program, which he named **Wolf Timbers** (866-874-9653).

It operates on about 30 acres on a remote wooded hillside. A path leads you down through the woods to an eight-foot-high fence. Once inside here you can see a smaller area, about one acre in size, that is also fenced in. In there are the wolves—three of them, two males and a female.

Bleachers and an elevated deck for wheelchairs outside the fence are as close as visitors get to the wolves. Marty instructs them not to make eye contact with the wolves (wolves perceive that as a threat), to be quiet (wolves are frightened by humans), and not to eat in front of them (he doesn't want wolves associating humans with food).

Marty asserts that there has never been a proven case of an unprovoked wolf attack on a human being. Reported attacks on pioneers were probably by packs of wild dogs, he says, not wolves. He also reminds visitors that a wolf is a wild animal and would make a lousy pet.

Sometimes Marty and his volunteers start to howl like a wolf, and the wolves join in. It's sort of a backwoods sing-along, wolf-style. The wolves seem to love it and become very active, leaping on fallen trees, throwing back their heads, and loosing a hair-raising howl. It's such a popular part of the attraction that Wolf Timbers offers special "Howlnights" during the year when you can come and join in.

A Cannon with Whitewalls

BRIGHTON

Brighton is just a crossroads, a wide spot in the highway between the village of Wellington on the east and the town of Bellevue on the west. But in the fervor following victory in World War II, local veterans wanted a memorial to their service and petitioned the government for a piece of equipment—a used tank, perhaps, or a fighter plane—something that would honor the men and women of the community who had answered their country's call to arms.

What they got was kind of a disappointment at first. It was a small cannon with two rather dingy black rubber tires. The cannon also needed a paint job. It was chipped and rusting, as though it had been lying around a supply yard somewhere (which it probably had).

Brighton at that time was mostly made up of farm folks, and farm folks know how to make do. It's a way of life. So they hid their disappointment, cleared a patch of land, raised a flagpole, and put in a cement foundation for the little cannon. It looked like thousands of other small community parks.

Which wasn't quite enough, apparently, for some local citizens.

Right after World War II everyone wanted their cars to have fancy white-sidewall tires. It was all the rage, especially with high school students. Some folks in Brighton say it must have been those high school students; perhaps some of the young veterans also helped. In any event, folks woke up one morning to find their cannon sporting bright white-sidewall tires. It did give the gun a rather jaunty look. Some even said the whitewalls sort of softened the image of war that the cannon fostered. Anyway, the whitewalls were left on the cannon, and today many passersby still do a double-take when they see what is perhaps the only cannon in America with whitewall tires.

The Brighton cannon can be seen at the intersection of State Routes 511 and 18.

A King Was Born Here

CADIZ

His neighbors in Cadiz weren't overly proud of Clark Gable until he became a big-time actor known as the "King of Hollywood." Even then, they let his birthplace be torn down.

William Clark Gable was born on February 1, 1901, in an upstairs apartment of a home on Charleston Street. Five months after his birth, the family moved to a house on Lincoln Avenue.

Gable grew up in Harrison County, and when he was 17 he moved with his father first to Akron to work in the rubber industry and later out west to try his hand in the oil fields. Then he got discovered and went on to have a movie career that lasted several decades.

Even after Gable's death in the 1960s, little was done to celebrate his connection to Cadiz. His birthplace had been razed, and local folks were hard pressed to even point out where it had been.

Cadiz isn't shy about honoring folks. For a while in the early part of the last century, General George Armstrong Custer was the favorite son of Cadiz—even though he was actually born in New Rumley. Custer was memorialized in a hotel that bore his name, as well as by several businesses. (The citizens of New Rumley put a large statue of Custer on the site where his house once stood—it seems the birthplaces of historical figures aren't highly prized in Harrison County.)

Cadiz began to think about capitalizing on one of their famous native sons in the early 1980s, when the town was suffering economically because of a downturn in demand for high-sulfur coal. A local group started holding a birthday celebration to honor Gable. It raised enough funds to buy a memorial marker to put on the property where Gable's birthplace once stood.

They chose the birthplace despite the fact that Gable had lived in the house for only about five months and had no memories of it. And despite the fact that his boyhood home, where he did spend most of his youth, was still standing nearby, the local group decided to launch a campaign to rebuild the Gable birthplace.

Many birthday parties later, the house was re-created. They even convinced Gable's only son, John Clark Gable, to come from California to cut the

Is this Clark Gable's busboy jacket?

ribbon and tour the reconstructed four-room, second-floor apartment now known as the **Clark Gable Foundation** (138 Charleston St., Cadiz; 740-942-4989).

Maybe It's Someting About the Water in Harrison County

CADIZ

Maybe it's something in the water, but a whole lot of famous or near-famous people have been born in, or lived in, Harrison County, Ohio. Leading the pack is Clark Gable (see "A King Was Born Here"). Way back in 1938, a national radio show proclaimed Cadiz the "Proudest Little Town in America" because they had such a large number of well-known people who started their lives there.

The list included General George Armstrong Custer; Thomas Ward Custer (the only man to ever win two Congressional Medals of Honor in the same war); Edwin Stanton (Lincoln's secretary of war); Denton T. (Cy) Young (Baseball Hall of Fame pitcher); General Thomas M. Vincent (Civil War general who delivered news of Lincoln's death to Vice President Andrew Johnson, and later ambassador to Japan); Ed Onslow (another Baseball Hall of Famer); and Edward Rensi (one time president of McDonald's).

There are even more names, but you get the idea. This is fertile ground for the birth of people who are destined to be leaders. Problem is, most of them left and never returned to their roots.

The **Harrison County Courthouse** (100 W. Market St., on the square in Cadiz) displays plaques honoring many famous local sons and daughters.

The Silver Spade

CADIZ

The Silver Spade, one of the largest dragline shovels in the world, is still working in the coalfields of Harrison County.

How large is it? Well, it weighs fourteen million pounds. Its shovel, in a single bite, can scoop up to 105 cubic yards—about 158 tons—of dirt and rock. Its boom stretches 200 feet into the air (the height of the first drop on Cedar Point's Magnum roller coaster). It could stand on the 50-yard line of a football field, pick up 158 tons in one end zone, swing it across the entire football field in one motion, and place it 45 feet beyond the goalpost at the opposite end. Pretty darn large.

The Silver Spade was built in the Ohio coalfields and started operating in November, 1965. Its job is to remove dirt and rock above coal seams so that miners can more easily reach the coal.

Most people can't appreciate its size, because you can only see the Silver Spade occasionally from the roadside, working far in the distance. But once in a while it changes location and has to cross a road. Then, when it dwarfs large trucks and even the roadway itself, you see just how big it really is.

The **Harrison Coal and Reclamation Park** (P.O. Box 403, Cadiz, OH 43907) has already preserved a sizable collection of big earthmoving equipment and hopes to crown its display with the Silver Spade when its working days are over. The HCRP operates a museum that is open for guided tours—"at your own risk," they emphasize.

Q: Why did the Silver Spade cross the road?
A: Does a 14-million-pound vehicle need a reason?

First Ladies' Library

CANTON

Every U.S. president since Rutherford B. Hayes has had a presidential library dedicated to him. But what about their wives?

First ladies, of course, aren't elected. But they do happen to be the bed-mates of presidents, and that gives them an extraordinary perspective on history. What if a first lady kept a diary? What if she didn't agree with her husband? What if she suspected him of "fooling around"? Well, the possibilities are endless, but the reality is that taxpayers or even large donors probably wouldn't spend the money to build twin libraries or museums for a first couple.

Well, now they don't have to. We have the **National First Ladies' Library** (331 Market Ave. S., Canton; 330-452-0876). It's located in the childhood home of former first lady Ida McKinley, wife of our 25th president, William McKinley.

Ida Saxton McKinley lived in this home before and after she married William McKinley. In fact it's the only home connected with the McKinleys still standing in Canton. The home they were living in when he was elected president was torn down years ago to make way for a hospital, and today the site is home to the county library.

The National First Ladies' Library operates an Internet site that collects all the information that can be found about the women who once served as first ladies of the land. The actual library contains a large assortment of books, many out of print, that have been written about the women. There is also a museum that contains a collection of photos, paintings, and other memorabilia belonging to the first ladies.

Johnny Carson's DeLorean

CANTON

You can find the darnedest things in museums. At the **Canton Classic Car Museum** (555 Market Ave. S., Canton; 330-455-3603), the second-largest antique car museum in Ohio, one of the top attractions is not an antique but a curiosity.

It's the 1981 stainless steel DeLorean once used by TV entertainer Johnny Carson.

And it's not just any DeLorean. It's a "$500,000" model presented to the late-night talk-show host in gratitude for his investments in the DeLorean Company.

In fact it's the very same gull-winged sports car that Carson was driving when he was arrested for drunken driving in Los Angeles in October of 1982. Although he pleaded no contest, the judge sentenced him to three years probation, fined him $603, and suspended his driving privileges until he completed a driver improvement course.

The car was seized as corporate property when the DeLorean Company went into receivership. It was sold at auction and is on loan to the Canton Classic Car Museum.

The First Highway

CANTON

Next time you sit cursing in bumper-to-bumper traffic on the highway, remember that at one time there weren't even any interstates.

If, say, you wanted to go from the east coast to the west coast, once you left the city streets you found yourself at first on gravel and then ordinary mud paths that were supposed to be roads. Many were unmarked, and it was anyone's guess exactly where you were or where you were headed.

As you got farther west, farther away from the cities and the farms, the roads just stopped, and, at the very best, you might have a trail or smooth area to follow. In short, driving was pretty much restricted to the cities, where they at least had paved streets.

A man by the name of Carl Fisher wanted to change all that. Fisher was president of an Indiana firm called Prest-O-Lite (he was also creator of the Indianapolis Motor Speedway).

Fisher wanted to build a coast-to-coast rock road, and to do it he turned to two Ohio men: Frank Seiberling, president of Goodyear in Akron, and Henry Joy, president of the Packard Motor Car Company, which had started in Warren. Joy wanted to name the highway in honor of Abraham Lincoln. He was named president of the Lincoln Highway Association in 1913.

What they did was lay out a series of roads that connected cities, towns, and villages across 3,389 miles of America. It stretched from Times Square in New York City to Lincoln Park in San Francisco. It was to be America's first coast-to-coast paved highway. Building it wasn't easy. States, towns, and villages had to cooperate, and there was the question of who would pay for it. But it finally happened, and while a far cry from today's wide interstate expanses, it did tie the country together and provide the first transcontinental highway. It twisted and turned, was only two narrow lanes in many places, and was made of bricks or sometimes just gravel, but it was a highway, and it was marked. You could travel and see occasional markers identifying the highway to reassure you that you were not lost.

The Ohio section of the highway passed through 11 Ohio counties and seven county seats. In 1928, Boy Scouts in Ohio placed identifying cement markers along the highway. Only three remain today; they can be seen along U.S. Route 30 in East Canton, Mifflin, and near Dalton. If you are driving along U.S. Route 30 today and notice a road or highway sign that says "Lincoln Way" or "Lincoln Road," it's part of the original Lincoln Highway that went coast to coast.

The Little Car from Ohio

CANTON

Right after World War II a couple of guys in Athens, Ohio, decided they wanted to create a new kind of automobile, one that was small and inexpensive and could be bought direct from the factory. They created the King Midget.

Believe it or not, their Midget Motors Corporation was the sixth largest manufacturer of automobiles in the United States for a number of years.

Claud Dry and Dale Orcutt wanted to design a car that anyone could afford. Their first was just a one-passenger model with a single-cylinder engine. Later versions seated two and were powered by 7.5 horsepower—about the same as garden tractors today.

They also added one other little touch. No dealers. You had to come to the factory to buy the car.

The later version of the car closely resembled early golf carts. In fact, they made a model that could be adapted to the golf course, and as an accessory you could have two golf-bag racks installed, and extra-wide tires for traveling over the turf.

Surprisingly, the little car company survived for nearly 25 years, going through several owners and finally stopping production in 1970.

Today there are several King Midget automobile clubs, and you

can see a typical model on display at the **Canton Classic Car Museum** (555 Market Ave. S., Canton; 330-455-3603).

Dead Man Talking

CANTON

U.S. president William McKinley may be dead, but he's still talking. The **McKinley Museum and National Memorial** (800 McKinley Monument Dr., Canton; 330-455-7043) has life-size animatronic versions of President and Mrs. McKinley. Enter a large second-floor room of this Victorian home, and you'll see what appears to be a couple of mannequins, frozen in time. But trigger an invisible beam and these lifelike First Figures start chatting away. It can be pretty unsettling for

*The McKinleys patiently wait for their chance
to startle another unsuspecting visitor.*

a first-time visitor. President McKinley comes alive!

The Fighting McCooks

CARROLLTON

Some families are just born to fight. I don't mean with each other. They're the kind of people that we are all very grateful for every time a war comes along.

Through the years there have been many cases of family members going off to war together. (Among the best known are the five Sullivan brothers who joined the Navy in World War II and all died while fighting on the same ship.) But the contributions of one Ohio family during the Civil War are hard to beat.

Major Daniel McCook of Carrollton went off to war accompanied by his nine sons and five nephews. They were rightly called "The Fighting McCooks."

Five members of the family became generals during the war.

Daniel McCook, at age 63, lost his life in the war; a son, Latimer McCook, a doctor, died of wounds he received in the war; another son, Charles McCook, also was killed in battle.

A son, Edwin Stanton McCook, one of the five promoted to general, became acting governor of Dakota and was assassinated there in 1873.

You can see the home and hear the story of the Fighting McCooks at the **McCook House and Civil War Museum** (Carroll County Historical Society, on the square in Carrollton; 800-600-7172).

The Blue Hole

CASTALIA

The Blue Hole in Castalia has been a bona fide Ohio tourist attraction for many years.

And it's just a hole in the ground, full of water. But people from all over America have paid money to come and see it.

What is so special about this particular hole in the ground? Maybe it's that everything in the hole, including the water, is sort of a blue-green color. Also, local legend has it that the hole has no bottom—anything that falls in just keeps right on going into the center of the earth.

The fact is, nobody has yet figured out just where the water does come from. The actual depth of the Blue Hole is about 70 feet. Through a small hole at the bottom, water from an underground source pushes its way to the surface. Water that has no life in it—no oxygen—and that is constantly at 48 degrees, winter and summer. The Blue Hole never freezes.

About 7,500 gallons of that water gush from the earth every minute, filling both the Blue Hole and other nearby cavities and also spawning Cold Creek (which eventually runs into Lake Erie at Sandusky Bay).

The Blue Hole is owned by a local fishing club that operated the attraction for several years as a sort of side business. Dwindling admission receipts and the cost of complying with the Americans with Disabilities Act proved too high, so the park around the Blue Hole was closed.

Fans of the legendary Blue Hole were saddened when the fishing club that owned it closed it to visitors. Then a new Blue Hole popped up right next door, and now natural mystery is back in business.

That seemed to be the end of the story. The Blue Hole was still there, behind locked gates still pumping 7,500 gallons of water a minute into Lake Erie, but the public could not see it.

Then came a discovery. The state of Ohio had purchased a fish hatchery next to the Blue Hole property to raise trout and other fish for Ohio streams. Part of the purchase included a second Blue Hole, about the same size as the original. The grass around it was mowed, some decking was put down on the marshy edges of the spring, and a new Blue Hole is now open to the public.

The water, which contains lime, soda, magnesia, and iron (that's what causes the blue color) encrusts just about everything, including moss and tree stumps that fall into the pool.

You can see the new Blue Hole year round Monday through Friday from 8 a.m. until 3 p.m. at **Castalia Fish Hatchery** (7018 Home-gardner Rd., Castalia; 419-684-7499).

UNUSUAL GOVERNORS

Ohio's Forgotten Governor

John Brown of Medina—the governor, not the abolitionist—is part of the curious history of Ohio.

Brown, a one time state highway patrolman, served overseas as an officer in the Coast Guard in World War II. Following his return to civilian life, like many veterans he got involved in politics. After a term as mayor of Medina, he ran for lieutenant governor of Ohio and won. It looked like he was on a fast track to becoming the next governor of Ohio. In those days the governor and the lieutenant governor could be from different parties. And this was the case in 1956, when Brown made his bid for governor. Then governor Frank Lausche was a Democrat, while Brown was a Republican. Lausche decided to run for the U.S. Senate that year, opening up the governor's job. Brown ran for the Republican nomination, but lost to C. William O'Neil, another power in the Republican party. Lausche went on to win his Senate race, and O'Neil won the governor's office.

Much to Brown's surprise, Lausche decided to resign the governor's office on the third day of 1957, to give himself a chance to be sworn in early in the Senate, thereby gaining some prized seniority. O'Neil wasn't to be sworn in as governor until January 14, when the governor's term begins. That meant that Brown became governor of Ohio for 11 days.

In most cases like this, the "temporary" governor just acts as a caretaker and makes very few waves until the duly elected successor takes over. John Brown was a different kind of caretaker. He decided that if he was to be governor of Ohio in name, he would be governor in fact as well.

He and his wife moved into the governor's mansion and immediately held a reception to which the public was invited. (They attended in droves.)

He addressed the legislature and outlined his concerns about the need for more school funds and for soil conservation, and he warned of future problems that would be created by the urbanization of the countryside. He took it upon himself to mediate a strike against a telephone company in Portsmouth, and got a settlement. And he commuted four first-degree murder convictions. Finally, he got a bill passed giving raises to state employees. Quite a busy 11 days for a "caretaker" governor.

When January 14 came, he moved out of the governor's mansion and went back to Medina to open a busi-ness. But in 1959 he was back, elected as a state representative from Medina; then in 1961 he was elected as a state senator from his district. In 1963 he went back to the Statehouse as lieu-tenant governor, serving until 1971. While he let it be known that he would like to make another run for governor, it never happened.

You can see a portrait of our 58th governor, John Brown, in the State-house in Columbus.

Ohio's First Woman Governor

Since Ohio became a state in 1803 we have had more than 67 governors and only one of them was a woman and our only woman governor held that office for a total of only 11 days.

Nancy Putnam Hollister was sworn in as our 66th governor on Thursday, December 31, 1998. She left office on January 11, 1999, when newly elected governor Robert A. Taft took over.

How did it all happen? Hollister had been serving as lieutenant governor under former governor George Voinovich. When Voinovich ran for the U.S. Senate and won, he had a chance to get a leg up on the competition and win some precious Senate seniority by resigning before the newly elected governor took over and taking his oath of office in the Senate on January 1.

So when Voinovich resigned, Nancy Hollister became our first woman gov-ernor. She made no appointments and just served as a caretaker until January 11, until newly elected governor Bob Taft took over. She did move into the state-owned governor's mansion (called "the residence" by governors who don't like to let people know they live in a mansion) for security reasons. However, she later admitted she didn't move any furniture in, or change any-thing in the mansion. She said she just lived out of her overnight bag while there.

A portrait of Governor Hollister hangs in the Statehouse in Columbus.

The Father of CB Radio
CLEVELAND

Timing is everything.

Al Gross of Cleveland was a tinkerer. He was fascinated by radio. While he was in his teens he was a ham radio operator and invented the first walkie-talkie two-way radio. (It inspired Chester Gould, creator of the cartoon strip *Dick Tracy* to include a wrist-mounted two-way radio in the comic strip.)

During World War II, Gross worked for military intelligence and developed two-way radios used by spies and resistance fighters. After the war, Gross thought that there should be a wireless radio for the common man, so he invented that, too: citizens band, or CB, radio.

In 1949, a friend at a hospital told him about the problem of reaching doctors by telephone. Gross went to his workbench and came up with the first pager. But when he attended a conference of physicians that year, expecting them to make this invention a smashing success, he was met with a total lack of interest. One doctor told him that he couldn't understand why any physician would want such a product—especially on the golf links on their afternoon off. The first pager was a commercial flop. It was too far ahead of its time.

It was much the same story with Gross's other inventions. His key copyrights expired in early 1970, long before the electronic revolution. So when CB radios became the rage, Gross didn't see a penny. Back in the 1950s, he tried to interest telephone companies in an idea he had for a wireless mobile phone. They didn't listen.

Al Gross was always the right man, with the right invention . . . at the wrong time.

So other than lots of awards and plaques that call him the "father of two-way radio," he didn't get much out of his inventions, and Al Gross spent his life working for other people.

Balto the Wonder Dog

CLEVELAND

There's a statue of Balto the Wonder Dog in New York's Central Park, but Cleveland's got the real thing.

He's dead, of course. In fact, he's been dead since 1933, when he passed on at the Cleveland Zoo. But he's still standing at the ready in the **Cleveland Museum of Natural History** (1 Wade Oval, Cleveland; 216-231-4600).

Who was Balto, and why was he so famous?

In 1925, Balto was just another Alaskan sled dog, when an epidemic of diphtheria broke out in Nome. Several children had died of the disease, and local doctors put out a radio message asking for life-saving antitoxin serum. It was midwinter, and in those days sled-dog teams were still relied on for transportation.

A hospital in Anchorage had the serum, but the state was in the midst of a blizzard. The serum went by train as far it could go, then sled-dog teams were to try relaying the precious medicine the rest of the way to Nome. It was a wild trip. Temperatures were at nearly 50-below zero, and the wind was so vicious that dog-sled drivers could hardly see the trail.

The last 56 miles of the trip were the most severe. They had to pass over a frozen lake, with no markers to guide them. In addition, Gunnar Kaasen, the driver, was rendered temporarily blind by the blowing snow particles and so had to rely totally on the directional instinct of his lead dog—Balto.

The team made it in time to save many children. The story was picked up by news media around the world, and the dogs, especially Balto, became international heroes.

So many people wanted to see the spunky little dogs that it was arranged for them to tour the United States. But fame is fleeting, and before they got back home the tour ran out of money. The dogs were sold to a vaudeville promoter, and that seemed to be the end of the story—until in 1927 Cleveland businessman George Kimble, visiting California, found the dogs on display in a rundown, filthy exhibition hall. The dogs were sick and ill-kept. Kimble came back to Cleveland and started a campaign to save the animals. Cleveland schoolchildren donated pennies and nickels, and residents also chipped in to raise $2,000, a very large sum in those days. It was the asking price for Balto and the team. They were brought back to Cleveland and given a home at the Cleveland Zoo for the rest of their lives.

Balto died in 1933, and, in a tribute to his heroism, he was stuffed and mounted and put on display at the Cleveland Museum of Natural History.

Oh, and in death he finally did get back home—briefly. He was loaned to Alaska a couple of years ago to be part of a program about the rescue. But after a short visit Balto came back to Cleveland.

Today he only makes occasional appearances for groups of youngsters, usually around the anniversary of the great rescue. Call the museum to see if Balto is scheduled to be on the job.

Free Stamp

CLEVELAND

One person's art is another person's . . . well, you finish the sentence.

Not all of us share the same aesthetic.

Take, for instance, the world's largest rubber stamp, er, priceless work of art—that stands in the shadow of Cleveland City Hall.

When the Standard Oil Company was building its headquarters on Cleveland's Public Square, it commissioned artist Claes Oldenburg to create a 28-foot-tall, 48-foot-wide steel sculpture shaped like a rubber office stamp, with the word "Free" on top, as the centerpiece of the new building's lobby. Before the stamp could be delivered, though, Standard Oil was sold to BP, and the new British management didn't seem to like the idea of having it anywhere near the building.

So the stamp was placed in storage in Indiana, and there it lay, forgotten, for the next seven years. Forgotten, that is, except by the BP officials who had to authorize the storage fees each month. In 1991 BP had finally had enough, and they offered to donate *Free Stamp* to the city of Cleveland as public art.

But city officials said, "No thanks"—they didn't like it much, either. Their attitude changed, however, when BP upped the ante and offered not only to give the stamp to the city but to pay for its installation, too. Suddenly it was much more attractive. And you might say that's how Cleveland got *Free Stamp* for free.

Free Stamp sits in **Willard Park** (Lakeside Ave., just east of City Hall, Cleveland).

Eliot Ness Comes Home

CLEVELAND

Eliot Ness, the "untouchable" from the 1950s TV series, was a real person and, for a part of his life, an Ohioan. And now he's spending eternity here.

Most of us associate Ness with Al Capone and the gangsters of 1920s Chicago. To be sure, Ness was there, but most of the stories we saw on television about Eliot Ness were just that, stories—a writer's fantasy, made up over the objections of Ness, who wanted just the facts told. Ness worked hard to bring down Capone, but the job was done mostly by accountants in the treasury department. The real Eliot Ness probably never carried a Thompson submachine gun, either. His career in Chicago was rather routine and attracted very little news media attention.

When Ness was done in Chicago, he came to Cleveland and became the city's safety director. He cleaned up the police department, ousting cops that were on the take, and he took on street gangs that were running out of control. He even cut traffic deaths enough to win awards for the city. But then he inexplicably left town to work for the government again, at the height of his popularity, rejecting calls that he run for mayor in 1941. (He did come back in 1946 and, against the advice of his friends tried to run for mayor, but by then too many years had gone by; he was badly beaten.) All in all, Ness did a far better job in Cleveland, and probably accomplished more good in Ohio, than he ever did in Chicago, but that is not what he is remembered for.

In fact, Ness never saw himself become famous. He died of a heart attack in 1957, just as the book *The Untouchables* was being published. He was so uncertain that the book would be popular that he sold the rights to his story for just $300. He died never knowing that Hollywood was about to make him into a legend. Desilu Studios bought the story, and in 1959, with actor Robert Stack as Ness, they brought the story to the small screen.

Eliot died nearly broke, and at his request he was cremated. A few years later his ashes were joined by those of his last wife, Elisabeth, and adopted son, Robert, when they passed away. The three boxes of cremains wound up in the northern Ohio garage of a Ness family friend.

They sat there for nearly 40 years until Rebecca McFarland, a research librarian and vice president of the Cleveland Police Historical Society, got a tip. She managed to locate the family friend and convinced him to donate the remains to the Police Museum on condition that they "disperse" the remains over water.

A plot at Lake View Cemetery was donated, and permission granted to spread the remains over Wade Lake there. A monument was also donated, and on Wednesday, September 10, 1997, Eliot Ness officially and finally came home to Cleveland as funeral services were held at the cemetery.

Ness the legend made millions of dollars for Hollywood, but Ness the man never benefited from his fame.

Besides the memorial in **Lake View Cemetery** (12316 Euclid Ave., Cleveland; 216-421-2665), you can also see an exhibit of some of Eliot Ness's personal belongings at the **Cleveland Police Historical Society and Museum** (Justice Center, 1300 Ontario St., Cleveland; 216-623-5055).

The Crime Eliot Ness Couldn't Solve

CLEVELAND

Among Ohio's most infamous unsolved crimes were the Torso Murders in Cleveland during the 1930s.

They baffled crime-fighter Eliot Ness, who was then the city's safety director. The murders eventually stopped, though no one was ever charged. There were 13 murders in all, mostly of unidentified people. All were decapitated and dismembered, possibly while they were still alive. The grisly chain of murders went on for four years.

In his desperation to solve the mystery, Ness took an unusual step.

In 1936 the Great Lakes Exposition, a sort of world's fair, was being held in Cleveland, and thousands of tourists were flocking to the city.

Ness was in the midst of trying to identify one of the most recent victims, a man in his twenties, who had been decapitated like the rest. He ordered a plaster mask made of the severed head and put it on display at the Great Lakes Exposition in hopes that someone would recognize the man. Although more than 100,000 people gawked at the gruesome display, no one identified him.

That plaster head is still on display (along with the heads of three other victims) at the **Cleveland Police Historical Society and Museum** (Justice Center, 1300 Ontario St., Cleveland; 216-623-5055). The crimes are still officially unsolved.

A plaster head of the last victim is part of the Cleveland Police Historical Society and Museum's "Torso Murder" collection.

One of the Largest Exhibition Buildings in the World
CLEVELAND

It's so big that you could drive a jumbo jet through the doors and onto the floor.

It's so big it has its own railroad spur; the line runs right through the center of the building.

It's so big, a giant Ferris wheel fits inside (just poking out through the roof).

It's the International Exposition Center—the I-X Center, for short. With nearly a million square feet of continuous exhibition space, the giant building is one of the largest single-structure exhibition buildings in the entire world.

Exhibitors love it, visitors like its easy access and convenient parking. You'd think Clevelanders would be plenty proud of owning such a facility.

The city can't wait to tear it down. They want the land for a runway expansion at neighboring Cleveland Hopkins Airport.

The I-X Center was erected back in 1942, specifically for building giant B-29 Superfortress bombers. Hence the big doors and enormous indoor space. At its peak it employed 15,000 workers.

During the Korean War, it was operated by General Motors, and army tanks were built there.

It was finally declared surplus in 1972, and the government sold the building in 1977 to the Park Corporation of Charleston, West Virginia, which in 1985 came up with the concept of making the old plant into a giant exhibition center. The hall became home to giant trade shows.

The land the building stands on, however, has been argued over for years. The city of Brookpark owned it (and raked in the taxes from it). The city of Cleveland wanted it for their airport. The two bickering burgs finally struck a deal in 2001, and the **I-X Center** (6200 Riverside Drive, Cleveland; 800-795-9690) is doomed to destruction around 2015.

Life Savers
CLEVELAND

If you've ever enjoyed those little round candies with the hole in the middle, you can thank an Ohioan.

Back in 1891, Clarence Crane started manufacturing chocolates in Cleveland. But in those pre-air-conditioning days, chocolate sales sagged in the summer. (Chocolate gets pretty messy above 80 degrees.) Crane began experimenting with hard candy shaped like little life preservers. He called them Crane's Pep-O-Mint Life Savers. They became popular, and soon he was selling them year round.

A New York company bought out Crane's Life Savers trademark in 1913, paying him just $2,900 for the name and the recipe.

But don't feel too sorry for Clarence. His chocolate business continued to grow nationwide, making him very successful by the time of his death in 1931.

He also was the father of poet Hart Crane.

The Only Major League Baseball Player Killed on the Field
CLEVELAND

Raymond Chapman holds the distinction of being the only major league professional baseball player to be killed while playing the game.

Chapman, who played shortstop for the Cleveland Indians from 1912 to 1920, was hit by a ball pitched by Carl Mays of the New York Yankees, at the Polo Grounds on August 16, 1920. He died 12 hours later in a New York hospital. His death came at a time when the Indians were making their first real bid for a championship. Thousands turned out for his funeral at St. John Cathedral in downtown Cleveland.

His teammates dedicated the rest of the season to him and went on to win their first league and world championships.

Chapman is buried in **Lake View Cemetery** (12316 Euclid Ave., Cleveland; 216-421-2665), where baseball fans decorate his grave each year with baseball bats, gloves, and Cleveland Indians memorabilia.

Rock and Roll–Born in Ohio?

CLEVELAND

A lot of people claim that rock and roll was born in Ohio. It wasn't, but the name, at least, was coined there—by Cleveland disk jockey Alan Freed.

Freed was working at WXEL-TV (forerunner of FOX 8 TV) in 1951 when record store owner Leo Mintz talked him into playing some rhythm-and-blues records on WJW radio. (At that time rhythm and blues was associated solely with African-Americans.) Freed, calling himself "Moondog," took over the show and was a hit.

In March of 1952 Freed sponsored a dance, called the Moondog Coronation Ball, at the 10,000-seat Cleveland Arena. He invited many of the black rhythm-and-blues performers to entertain. An estimated crowd of nearly 20,000 showed up, the overflow crowd crashed the gates, and police had to cancel the dance. Nevertheless, this is considered the first rock concert.

In 1954, Freed moved on to New York City, where he staged another concert with many of the same performers, who were now called rock-and-roll artists. Within a month, the music industry was promoting rock-and-roll recordings across the country.

In the late 1950s Freed became embroiled in the payola scandal that shook up the radio business and was fired from his broadcasting jobs. He died in Palm Springs, California, in January of 1965. In 1986, Freed was among the original inductees into the **Rock and Roll Hall of Fame** (1 Key Plaza, Cleveland; 888-764-7625).

Rocket Man
CLEVELAND

Drivers on Cleveland's East Side often report seeing a large silver rocket ship zooming up on them in their rearview mirrors.

It's not a hallucination. It's Ron Heitman of South Euclid.

If they take a second look, nostalgic motorists may recognize the shiny rocket from its earlier days hanging on cables at Cleveland's long-gone Euclid Beach Park.

Back then, three rockets flew in circles around a tall tower. Each car could seat 12 people. The park closed in 1969, and in 1978 Heitman came across one of the 28-foot-long rocket cars, bought it, and put it in his garage, not sure what to do with it.

In the mid-1970s, he arrived at the obvious conclusion: add a souped-up 455-horsepower Oldsmobile V8. With that, some wheels, and an enlarged front compartment big enough for a driver and a steering wheel, he had a distinctive vehicle that could carry 10 people and travel at a top speed of 136 miles per hour.

He originally planned only to show the car in a few auto shows, but it was such a success that he started getting calls (216-382-1616) to be in parades—including the Macy's Thanksgiving Day parade and the Indianapolis 500 parade. Then there were the wedding parties and others that wanted to rent the car. He's become so busy with the vehicle that he finally tracked down another of the original rocket cars and has built his second rocketmobile.

The Only Fully Intact WWII Submersible

CLEVELAND

If we ever go to war with Canada, Ohio is ready.

We have the only fully intact, nearly operational World War II fleet submarine, the *U.S.S. Cod* (docked near the E. 9th St. pier, open May–Sep.).

Of course the shallow depth of Lake Erie might make maneuvering difficult. But on the other hand, since the most threatening boat on the Canadian side is probably a fishing trawler, odds are we won't have to try it.

The *Cod* has called the Cleveland lakefront home since 1959, when it was towed to Ohio to become a Naval Reserve training vessel. It was decommissioned in 1954, stricken from the navy's official inventory in 1971, and seemed headed for the scrap pile when a group of Clevelanders petitioned the navy to give them the ship for use as a World War II memorial.

The navy wasn't convinced until Parma Heights restaurant owner Johnny Tarr entered the picture. Tarr, a Hungarian immigrant who had fought for Germany in the war, turned over his restaurant one weekend to the sub preservation committee. He donated the food and labor; the proceeds went to the committee. It wasn't only the money, it was the publicity the act attracted that finally did the trick. On January 25, 1976, the navy turned the *U.S.S. Cod* over to the Cleveland Coordinating Committee to Save the Cod, allowing it to become a memorial ship.

By the way, the *Cod* is an authentic war veteran. It sank more than a dozen enemy ships, including the Japanese destroyer *Karukaya*, in 1944, and also rescued the crew of a Dutch submarine that had to be abandoned in the South China Sea in 1945.

There's an interesting bit of trivia about the *Cod*. There was one piece of machinery aboard so important that the crew considered it impossible to patrol without. An ice-cream machine.

It may sound silly, but to young men crammed into small spaces, living under the sea for weeks and months at a time, ice cream was a real morale builder. The ice-cream maker on the *U.S.S. Cod* had been inoperable since the ship was mothballed in the 1950s. But in keeping with efforts to restore the ship as nearly as possible to its original condition, curator John Fakan worked out a deal with Lorain County vocational students. (They fixed the machine, and ate the first batch of ice cream it produced in 50 years.) Ironically, now that it's back on the sub, the ice-cream maker may never be used again, because it's in a museum. (By the way, the U.S. navy was the only navy in the world to put ice-cream machines on submarines in World War II.)

When Irish Eyes Are Smiling
CLEVELAND

Probably the most famous and popular Irish melody in the world was written by a Cleveland native who had never been to Ireland.

Ernest R. Ball, the composer of "When Irish Eyes Are Smiling," also wrote another Irish melody that we frequently hear on St. Patrick's Day, "Mother Machree," and he penned "A Little Bit of Heaven," another tune much loved by the Irish.

Ball never got to see the Emerald Isle. He died of a heart attack in 1927 and was buried in Lake View Cemetery (12316 Euclid Ave., Cleveland; 216-421-2665).

The Man Behind the Trophy
CLEVELAND

The Hiesman Trophy has been awarded to the best player in college football annually since 1935. I suspect there are more than a few people (including some of its recipients) who have no idea who it is named after.

In 1869, John William Heisman was born in what is now Ohio City on Cleveland's West Side. He grew up to be both a football player and a coach. Among the schools he coached at was Oberlin College. Yes, that Oberlin College—the one that rarely wins today. Heisman also coached at more than a half-dozen major universities. He changed the face of football forever with such innovations as the forward pass, center snap of the football, audible signals to begin offensive play, and, some say, the creation of the "T" formation.

It was during his retirement years, while he was president of the New York Touchdown Club, that awards were handed out for the first time to the nation's best college football players. After his death, the main award was renamed in his honor and today is synonymous with the best of the best in football.

His birthplace in Ohio City has a historic marker (the home is privately owned).

Giant Body Parts and a See-Through Woman

CLEVELAND

One of the headliners at the **Health Museum of Cleveland** (8911 Euclid Ave., Cleveland; 216-231-5010) is Juno, the Transparent Talking Woman. The museum is also home to several oversized body parts: the Giant Ear, the Giant Eye, the Giant Hand, the Giant Nose . . . well, you get the idea. But hurry if you want to see the Giant Tooth; it is endangered by the museum's renovation plans. The tooth is, apparently, impacted, and will be destroyed when the floor is torn up for rebuilding sometime toward the end of 2001. Juno and more than a hundred other exhibits are expected to survive.

In keeping with the "Giant" theme, the museum also has a life-size model of the "Bates Baby," the largest baby born in the state of Ohio. (At birth, the Bates Baby had a head circumference of 19 inches, a length of 30 inches and weighed 23.75 pounds.) The museum will reopen sometime in 2003.

My! what big teeth you have, Giant Mouth.

North to Alaska ... On a Tractor?

DALTON

You've heard the expression "a slow boat to China"? Well, how about an antique tractor to Alaska?

Glen and Betty Martin of Dalton drove their 1950 John Deere tractor, nicknamed "Dandelion," from their tiny Wayne County community to Alaska (and back!)—9,500 miles, average speed about 13 miles per hour. They took this astounding trip in 1998, pulling a small trailer behind the tractor for emergency shelter when they could not find anyplace along the way to stay.

The Martins, both in their sixties at the time, said they decided to make the trip as a way to spread their Christian faith. They wrote a book about it: *To Alaska On A Tractor*.

Buried in Three States

DOVER

One of the really bad guys of the American Civil War was an Ohioan, William Clarke Quantrill of Dover. Now, he may be the only American who is buried in three graves, in three different states.

Quantrill always had a mean streak. It is said that as a child he nailed snakes to trees, shot pigs through the ears to hear them squeal, and tied cats together by their tails to watch them fight. Even walking through farmers' fields as a boy, he was known to stab horses and slice open cows. The kind of kid that even gives juvenile delinquents a bad name.

During the Civil War, Quantrill joined the Confederate army in Missouri and took off with his own band of irregulars, the feared "Quantrill's Raiders" that savaged towns and villages in the West. He is most often remembered for the August 1863 sacking of Lawrence, Kansas, when his troop of 450 men tore through the community, pillaging, burning, and killing men, women, and children.

His career finally ended when he was shot and captured in a battle in Kentucky. He died in a prison hospital in Louisville, Kentucky, and was buried in a cemetery there in 1865.

That's where *our* story actually begins.

In 1887, his mother and a boyhood friend visited the grave. She wanted the remains transferred to Dover, Ohio. The friend started digging, but when he unearthed the corpse he found it had disintegrated so badly that only a few bones and the skull were left. Most of his skeleton had turned to dust. Quantrill's mother identified the remains by a chipped tooth he had had since his youth.

The friend promised to transfer whatever bones he had found to Ohio, but he never got around to it.

The bones eventually ended up in the hands of the Kansas State Historical Society. In 1992, they gave one of Quantrill's arms and a shinbone to the Missouri Division of the Sons of Confederate Veterans, who buried them in the Confederate cemetery in Higginsville, Missouri. The skull went to the Dover Historical Society, which had it interred (in a fiberglass child's coffin) in the Fourth Street Cemetery. Before it went back in the ground, though, a cast-clay replica of Quantrill's head was made from the skull. This was displayed at the historical society for a while, but during the hot days of summer, water would bead on the surface, making it look like the head was alive and sweating. This disconcerted some visitors so much that the head was removed to a refrigerator. Now it is shown only on request.

Quantrill's replicated head was moved to this refrigerator because it was sweating too much.

Ohio's Master Carver
DOVER

Ernest "Mooney" Warther is known throughout the state as "Ohio's master carver." His is a remarkable story. His father died when he was only two. He was forced to quit school after the second grade to help provide for his family. At age 28, while working at a steel company, he started carving. He used soup bones from his wife's kitchen, then switched to walnut.

Warther decided to carve the history of the steam engine. He carved 64 locomotives. And these weren't just solid carvings, but in-

tricate models with moving parts. Tiny wheels turned, valves moved, pistons went up and down. Incredibly, he duplicated real locomotives in exact scale, down to the last rivet—without any plans and with essentially no formal education.

He carved, in miniature, the entire steel plant where he worked. He duplicated Abraham Lincoln's entire funeral train in ivory. He created ornate canes with caged balls in the handles. All done with a carving knife he had designed.

For amusement, Warther carved wooden pliers, first one pair, then a "tree" on which each branch folded out to form wooden pliers. The tree was a piece of black walnut 13 inches long, three-quarters of an inch wide, and five-eighths of an inch thick. Mooney calculated that if he made 31,000 cuts in the wood, he could create a tree with 511 pairs of working pliers when they were all folded out from the block of wood. He worked for nearly two months on the project, six to eight hours a day, before he completed it. It worked. It worked so well that it first appeared in *Ripley's Believe It Or Not* and then was loaned to the Ohio State Historical Museum in Columbus, where it was displayed for 14 years. Today it and many of Warther's other carvings are on display at the **Warther Museum** (331 Karl Ave., Dover; 330-343-7513).

Warther suffered a stroke while working on a steam locomotive called the *Lady Baltimore* and died in 1973 at the age of 87.

A Mortuary Museum/Bed and Breakfast

EAST LIVERPOOL

Here's one that really sets Ohio apart from other states. We have perhaps the only mortuary museum and bed and breakfast in the country.

It happened this way. Back in the mid 1930s, the infamous bank robber and murderer Charles "Pretty Boy" Floyd was number one on the FBI's most-wanted list. He was spotted while traveling near East Liverpool in October of 1934 and finally trapped by a posse of local lawmen and FBI agents on a farm near the location of what is now Beavercreek State Park. Floyd tried to run and was gunned down, bringing to an end his nefarious career.

Floyd's lifeless body was propped in the backseat of a police car and driven to Sturgis Funeral Home in East Liverpool. Frank A. Dawson, a funeral director working for Sturgis, took the bullet-riddled body into a basement preparation room for embalming.

Meanwhile word quickly spread through the small river town that "Pretty Boy" Floyd, America's number-one criminal, was dead, and that it had happened just outside of the city. Thousands of residents started to converge on the Sturgis Funeral Home. Everyone wanted to see the body. The crowd grew so large that an iron railing in front of the funeral home was torn from the ground. The lawn around the house was trampled.

The police, possibly fearing a riot, told funeral director Dawson to take the now-embalmed body into one of the viewing rooms and to let the people in.

Floyd was laid on a small bed in a center room on the first floor, his body partially covered by a blanket with only his shoulders and face visible. The doors were opened, and during the next three hours, from 8:30 until 11:30 that night, an estimated 10,000 people passed through the funeral home at a rate of about 50 per minute to catch a glimpse of the famous criminal.

The next morning Dawson shipped Floyd's body back to his family in Oklahoma, and things returned to normal in East Liverpool.

Today the former funeral home is owned by Frank C. Dawson, the son of the man who embalmed "Pretty Boy" Floyd. And the old Vic-

Amenities include private bath, in-room phones, and, of course, embalming exhibit and "Pretty Boy Floyd" death mask.

torian home is now a bed and breakfast. The **Sturgis House** (122 West 5th Street, East Liverpool; 330-382-0194) has six bedrooms with private bath, one with whirlpool. Other amenities include a phone in each room, as well as television . . . and, of course, a breakfast room where "Pretty Boy" Floyd was once laid out.

If you ask, you can see the museum in the basement. The room has been left as it was in the 1930s when "Pretty Boy" Floyd was brought here. There are pictures on the wall of Floyd before and after the embalming. You can see the table where the work was done. Some antique embalming equipment is also on display, as are several devices that were used under bodies to make them lie just so in a casket. If you're lucky, you might even get to meet Frank C. Dawson, who goes by the nickname "Digger." He and his family still operate a funeral home—just up the street.

A historical marker is located on Sprucevale Road, between East Liverpool and Rogers on the edge of Beavercreek State Park. The site is the former Conkle family farm, where Charles "Pretty Boy" Floyd was shot down by police and FBI agents. The marker was erected in 1993 by the East Liverpool Historical Society and the Ohio Historical Society. It was stolen in 1995 and discovered lying in a wooded lot in East Liverpool several weeks later. It was reerected and has been unmolested since then.

The Private Bridge over the Ohio River

EAST LIVERPOOL

To cross the Ohio River in East Liverpool, it will cost you either a nickel or four bits, depending on your mode of transportation.

Toll roads and toll bridges were once a way of life in our country. In the early days some bridges and even roads were privately owned, and people wanting to use them had to pay the toll or find some other way to cross the stream or swampy area.

But today about the only toll roads still operating are state-owned turnpikes and bridges. All, that is, but one down on the Ohio River.

The Newell Bridge that connects East Liverpool with Newell, West Virginia, was built way back in 1905 by the Homer Laughlin

China Company, and today is still wholly owned by the firm. They built the bridge because after starting their company in East Liverpool, on the Ohio side of the river, they decided to move to Newell, West Virginia, just across the river for a bigger riverfront location. The problem was how to get their employees, who mostly lived in Ohio, to work on time. The nearest public bridge was miles away.

So the decision was made to build a bridge over the Ohio River. Originally the bridge accommodated both trolleys and auto traffic, as well as pedestrians. Today the trolleys are gone, but nearly three thousand cars and trucks cross the bridge each day. Many of them carry Ohioans going across the bridge to reach the gambling casinos in West Virginia. And each car or truck pays 50 cents to cross the bridge. Pedestrians can walk across for only a nickel.

Otto Sirianni, the bridge manager, said that the tolls collected each year have been sufficient to maintain the bridge, and it has never had to be subsidized by anyone. The bridge floor was last replaced in 1954 but is inspected every spring for safety.

The Happiest Music on Earth
EUCLID

"The happiest music on earth" is what they call polka music. That must mean that the happiest musicians on earth are enshrined at the **National Cleveland-Style Polka Hall of Fame and Museum** (605 E. 222 St., Euclid; 216-261-3263).

Cleveland-style polka music has its roots in Slovenian folk music, but the influence of Cleveland's many other ethnic cultures has given it a distinctly American twist.

Songs like "Just Because Polka," "The Blue Skirt Waltz," "Slap Happy Polka," "I Wanna Call You Sweetheart Polka," "Little Fella Waltz," and "Old Timer's Polka" were born here.

The Polka King himself, Grammy award-winning Frankie Yankovic, is from Cleveland. He and other polka notables, like Walter Ostanek, Johnny Pecon, and the Vadnals—Frankie, Johnny, Richie, and Tony—are enshrined here.

Who Was the First President?
HARTSGROVE

Who was the first president of the United States? If you said George Washington, you might be wrong. At least as far as a Hartsgrove man is concerned.

When was the last time you saw John Hanson's picture on a $1 bill? Hanson was the first president of the United States elected under the Articles of Confederation. He was the first of eight men who served as president from 1781 until our current constitution was adopted in 1789. As most people know, George Washington was the first president elected under the constitution.

Nick Pahys, Jr., has spent most of his life studying the presidency, and he believes that all the presidents should be honored. So he has opened a presidential museum at his **Hartsgrove Emporium** (at the intersection of Rte.6 and Rte. 534, Hartsgrove; 440-474-5369) that includes the eight presidents elected under the Articles of Confederation. It may be the only one that does.

Pahys has made it his life's work to get recognition for John Hanson. He claims the man was completely ignored for at least 150 years, since he wasn't even mentioned in encyclopedias until 1929.

In case you were wondering, the other seven who served before George Washington were Elias Boudinot, Thomas Mifflin, Richard Henry Lee, John Hancock, Nathaniel Gorham, Arthur St. Clair, and Cyrus Griffin.

Harbingers of Spring: Buzzards

HINCKLEY

In California, tradition has it that every March 19 the swallows return to the mission of San Juan Capistrano. That signifies the coming of spring.

Heck, swallows are just little, bitty things. Here in Ohio spring brings real birds—turkey vultures with six-foot wingspans. They head for Hinckley Township.

Here's how this tradition supposedly got its start. On December 24, 1818, the good citizens of Hinckley decided to have a really big hunting party. About 600 men and boys formed a wide circle around the township and starting walking toward the center, shooting and

Keep your eyes on the sky. Or just wait for one to show up in the back of the park ranger's station wagon.

killing all the game they could find. When the day ended, the score was 300 deer, 17 wolves, 21 bears, and assorted fox, raccoons, and turkeys.

The hunters divvied up the best cuts of the meat, but they weren't very particular about what they did with the leftovers. Because it was winter, they just let the various carcasses lie on the ground to be covered by snow.

As long as the cold weather hung around and the snow kept falling, the scene probably looked just like one of those Currier and Ives paintings—a pioneer village under a mantle of white, smoke curling from the chimneys. However, when March rolled around so did the spring thaw, and as the snow melted and the temperatures rose, Hinckley didn't look or smell so good.

The smell soon brought huge flocks of turkey vultures (some call them buzzards), who started doing their thing. It was quite a picnic for them, and eventually the turkey vultures were so well fed that they decided to hang around for the rest of the summer. And they started returning to Hinckley every year on March 15.

It took them a while, but a few enterprising folks in Hinckley eventually found a way to capitalize on this creepy phenomenon. About 150 years later, they were looking for a way to raise funds for the school, and someone suggested hosting a pancake breakfast on the same day that the buzzards return. With proper publicity, maybe city folks would come out to see this marvel of nature—and buy a pancake breakfast.

Boy did they ever. Today, the annual return of the buzzards to Hinckley is reported in the papers, on radio, on television, and in cyberspace. News media swarm into the Hinckley Reservation of the Cleveland Metroparks to the "official" buzzard watching station. People from all over America come to witness the phenomenon. Some even dress up like buzzards. Most have field glasses and telescopes that they train on the sky, watching crows and robins dart through the distant tree line. The movement of any feathered creature brings cries of "I see them!" and "There they are!" and everyone rushes to the fence, straining to share in the excitement of the moment.

Personally, I have covered the buzzards' return to Hinckley about 20 times in the last 30 years and have yet to see a real live buzzard flying over Hinckley Ridge. I did see one in a cage at the school where the pancakes are served, but he got there in the back of a park ranger's station wagon. Nevertheless, you will still find dozens and dozens of people each year at the ridge viewing area who would take an oath on their mother's life that they did indeed see the buzzards flying back to Hinckley.

If you want to see for yourself, call the Hinckley Chamber of Commerce (330-278-2066) for dates of the pancake breakfast. The buzzards, of course, are supposed to be there on March 15. Buzzard Roost is located at the corner of State Road and West Drive in the Cleveland Metroparks Hinckley Reservation.

By the way, my colleague Dick Goddard, the dean of Ohio television weathermen, pointed out that buzzards are notorious for regurgitating while they are flying. So never stand under a group of flying buzzards and look up.

> Dozens and dozens of people each year would take an oath on their mother's life that they did indeed see the buzzards flying back to Hinckley.

MOTORCYCLE DEMOLITION DERBY

People these days seem to seek out ever more exciting and dangerous activities. If not personally, then at least vicariously. Ohioan Kevin Ruic supplies the latter kind of excitement to his home state and the rest of the world.

Ruic, you see, developed the sport of the Motorcycle Demolition Derby.

He had been involved in motorsports for years, having operated several racetracks in northern Ohio. But he was looking for newer, more exciting ways to attract a crowd.

One of his first ideas was an airplane demolition derby. But, he says, he only tried that one time.

"First of all, with all those propellers flying around, it was downright dangerous, not only for the contestants, but the audience as well," he remembers.

Then there was the cost of used airplanes. Even barely workable ones can be quite expensive, and they got chewed up so badly in the demolition derby that they couldn't be reused. So Ruic scratched Airplane Demolition Derby and looked in a completely different direction: Boat Demolition Derby.

Kevin Ruic doesn't discourage easily, it seems.

When one of his employees pointed out that to have a boat demolition derby, the boats would have to be in water, and that his racetrack was several miles from the nearest body of water, Ruic paused only briefly before having backhoes start to dig up the infield at his track to create Lake Ruic.

However, he hadn't considered one important factor about boats: when they crash, they leak, and when they leak, they often sink.

His boat demolition derby drew a sellout crowd. They saw a grand show. All but one of the boats sank to the bottom of Lake Ruic. (The sole surviving outboard motorboat was named, ironically, the Titanic.) Lake Ruic was filled in.

Ruic next turned his attention to motorcycles. Motorcycles? Surely no one would be insane enough to purposely crash one motorcycle into another one? But when he put out a call for contestants, he got so many entrants that he had to stage two heats to eliminate some of the would-be daredevils.

The rules? There are none, apparently. The idea is the last person astride the last motorcycle still running and moving is the winner.

It's been almost a quarter of a century now since he staged his first motorcycle demolition derby, and today Kevin Ruic and his son, Scott Ruic, have motorcycle demolition derbies all over America—from county fairs to motorsports speedways. Even ESPN has picked up on motorcycle demolition derbies. And it all started right here in Ohio.

World's Only Perambulator Museum

JEFFERSON

Twin sisters Judith Kaminski and Janet Pallo of Jefferson want to share their lifelong fascination with baby buggies.

Their **Victorian Perambulator Museum** (26 E. Cedar St., Jefferson; 440-576-9588) has the largest known collection of early wicker baby and doll carriages.

Modern foldable strollers give kids a lot more freedom, but some of the early baby buggies were pretty neat. For instance, one 1910 baby buggy was made to look like a Model T Ford. Another looks like a wicker gondola.

If you ever wondered what kids played with prior to the 20th century, the sisters also have a large collection of pre-1900 toys, sleds, and sleighs for children.

Open hours at the Perambulator Museum vary throughout the year, but it can also be toured by appointment. Just call first.

The Groovy Island

KELLEYS ISLAND

Kelleys Island in Lake Erie is truly groovy.

The island, the largest on the U.S. side of Lake Erie, displays very distinct grooves that were worn into it by a passing glacier.

This part of the earth was once covered by a giant ice floe. When it started to melt, around 18,000 years ago, the retreating ice dug deeply into the earth and stone that it passed over.

Kelleys Island is made up of solid limestone bedrock, and when the glacier passed over here it made very clear marks. One section of stone, about 430 feet long, 35 feet wide, and up to 15 feet deep, has escaped erosion and survived human interaction and still exists. Today it is fenced off as a national natural landmark.

Scientists think this grooved area was once much larger but was probably quarried away in the 19th century. It is located on the island's north side, adjacent to Kelleys Island State Park campground.

Now Hear This:

KENT

A casual remark during a interview with *National Hearing Aid Journal* was all it took to start the donations pouring in to Professor Kenneth Berger at Kent State University. Now that university has the largest collection of hearing aids in the world, housed in the **Kenneth W. Berger Hearing Aid Museum and Archives** (Music and Speech Building, Kent State University, Kent).

More than 3,000 different models of hearing aid are collected in large wooden cases in the hallway of the Speech Pathology and Audiology Clinic. The devices range from cumbersome vacuum-tube affairs to modern digital models. Many are demonstrated on mannequin heads (stylishly outfitted with period hats and scarves). One of the earliest exhibits is a 160-year-old silver ear trumpet from England. There are several examples of eyeglass hearing aids, which became popular when Eleanor Roosevelt was photographed using one.

The museum has been around since 1966, but it doesn't promote itself much. It is open for tours.

Queen Victoria's Bloomers
KENT

They probably won't show up in the pages of the Victoria's Secret catalog. They're not terribly sexy, or even attractive. But they're here in Ohio—an authentic pair of Queen Victoria's (blush) panties. Or, as they call them in England, knickers. Actually, I think they referred to them as bloomers in her day. Whatever, we've got 'em.

How did Queen Victoria's bloomers end up at the **Kent State University Fashion Museum** (Rockwell Hall, Kent State University, Kent; 330-672-3450)? They were part of a collection of 13 pieces of royal underwear and linens purchased by museum founders Shannon Rodgers and Jerry Silverman, probably at an auction in England.

Sadly for you voyeurs out there, the Queen's underwear is not on display at present. Museum staff said it is "resting," whatever that means. But it may be back on display in the future. And meanwhile you can see lots of other underwear (and outerwear) from all over the world. The collection contains more than 20,000 historic and contemporary world costumes.

The Non-Electric Store

KIDRON

Lehman's Hardware (One Lehman Circle, Kidron; 877-438-5346) claims to be the only "non-electric" hardware store in Ohio.

Located in the midst of Ohio's Amish country, the store has always carried the things the Amish use in their simple non-electric lifestyle. You can still buy a wood-burning cook stove here, brand new. You can also find things like oil lamps and lanterns, wringers, and hand-operated washing machines. You can even find a non-electric freezer here, powered by kerosene. It's like wandering through a general store from your great-grandmother's time.

Lehman's was a popular place during the Y2K scare at the end of 1999. City folks who thought they were going to lose their light and heat started a buying frenzy here, stocking up on wood-fired stoves, gasoline-powered washing machines, and the like. (Lehman's was more than a year behind in orders for the cook stoves at the height of the panic.) The Amish, who live this way all the time, just smiled and perhaps chuckled a bit at the actions of their panicky "Yankee" neighbors.

The Mailbox Factory

KIRTLAND

Wayne Burwell is a man who knows how to take a lemon and make lemonade out of it. He used to make his living plowing snow in the area around Kirtland, the heart of Ohio's snowbelt. Once in a while his plow would knock over a mailbox. As part of his service, Burwell would rebuild and replace the mailbox.

His work was so good that some folks started approaching him to build mailboxes for them *before* he knocked over their old ones. Then one day a customer asked Wayne if he could make the mailbox look like his earthmover. Wayne did, and a new business was born.

Today he heads up the **Mailbox Factory** (7857 Chardon Rd., Kirtland; 888-740-6245), and his mailboxes are unusual creations. One looks like a giant tooth being held up by a giant toothbrush. One's a replica of my 1959 Nash Metropolitan.

Big Mousetrap

LISBON

They say if you build a better mousetrap the world will beat a path to your door.

If that's the case, there must be a four-lane highway leading to the door of the Columbiana Career Center in Lisbon.

The students there set out to build the largest working model of the world's most popular mousetrap. And they did set a world's record in the Guinness book with a Victor-style mousetrap that was 9 feet, 10 inches long and 4 feet, 5 inches wide. And it actually works! If you were strong enough to hold back the spring, you could probably catch a bear in this baby.

The project was designed for the students to not only learn but to make some money for the student fund. The trap used to be on display at the school but has now been sold to a museum in Florida, and memories and a few pictures are all that is left at the school.

Longest Bascule Bridge in the U.S.
LORAIN

When you drive across the Charles Berry Memorial Bascule Bridge, over the Black River in Lorain, you're driving over the longest bascule, or lift, bridge in the United States and the second-largest in the world.

Built in 1940, it stretches 333 feet across the mouth of the river in front of what was once the Lorain Shipyards (owned by New York Yankees owner George Steinbrenner).

The bridge surface is a grid that you can see through when driving over it; an operator at the edge of the river can raise the two halves into an upright position when a large boat or tall sailboat wants to enter or exit the river.

The bridge, which is located on East Erie Avenue just east of Broadway in downtown Lorain, was named for Lorain native Corporal Charles Berry, USMC, who was posthumously awarded the Medal of Honor in World War II.

The Giant Easter Basket

LORAIN

Lorain's most notable landmark may be the giant Easter basket.

Lakeview Park, on West Erie Avenue, was laid out as a public works project in 1937, with a fountain in the middle of the rose garden (the lights changed color at night) and one of the best swimming beaches along Lake Erie.

Proud park officials wanted a fancy entrance at the end of the driveway. "Make something special," they told parks department mechanic David Shukait. He did.

He took some boards and built a long, curving form. He mixed up some concrete and started filling the molds. When he was done, he had dozens of what looked like giant stone bands, which he started assembling like a jigsaw puzzle.

And then it took shape: a huge concrete basket, 10 feet wide and nearly 9 feet high. Shukait painted it up to look like a gaily decorated flower basket, and because Easter was just around the corner but it was too early for flowers, he made nearly a dozen two-foot long concrete eggs and placed them in the basket. A tradition was born.

Nearly every Easter since, Lorain families have come to pay homage to the giant Easter basket and have their picture taken in front of it.

There were some problems. In the early years, teenagers got into the habit of swiping the eggs, which weighed nearly a hundred pounds each, sometimes having impromptu contests to see who could throw one the farthest.

So park officials redesigned the eggs, making them lighter, and now they are placed in the basket only during the week between Palm Sunday and Easter Sunday.

Now, I ask you, what's better than having a giant Easter basket? Having two, of course. Shukait actually made another, which is located at Oakwood Park, on Grove Avenue.

●

A Hollywood Wedding in Mansfield

MANSFIELD

Humphrey Bogart and Lauren Bacall were married in Ohio. On May 21, 1945, the Hollywood lovebirds tied the knot at Malabar Farm near Mansfield, then owned by Bogart's friend, Louis Bromfield.

Bogart was visiting Bromfield when the urge to marry struck. Bacall arrived in Mansfield by train. They went to the farm in a swirl of publicity and were planning to be married in the garden, but the number of curious onlookers forced them to hold the ceremony inside on the stairway to the second floor.

Bogie and Bacall trod these stairs on their way to the "honeymoon suite" with twin beds.

That evening, following the wedding, Bromfield showed them to the house's "honeymoon suite," a bedroom at the top of the stairs with two twin-sized beds in it.

Today the farm is a state park, and the home is very much as it was in the 1940s, including the Bogart-Bacall wedding suite. Tour guides note that both the twin beds had wheels on them, so they could easily be pushed together.

Malabar Farm State Park (4050 Bromfield Rd., Lucas; 419-892-2784) is open to the public year round.

Reformatory with a Gift Shop

MANSFIELD

Mansfield is home to one spooky-looking tourist attraction—the former Ohio State Reformatory. Built in 1886, this huge castle-like structure takes up more than 175,000 square feet and combines four architectural styles: Victorian, Gothic, Romanesque, and Queen Anne. It also houses the world's tallest freestanding steel cell block. It has six tiers and 12 ranges with more than 550 cells.

The prison operated until 1990, when it was finally closed, and a new prison opened about a mile away.

A local nonprofit historical society was formed to preserve the old prison, but before they could act the state started demolition, taking down the brooding walls that surrounded the main building. The society was able to save the rest of the structure and is now working to raise funds to restore it. In the meantime, Hollywood has discovered the old lockup; it has been used in several movies, including *The Shawshank Redemption*, *Air Force One*, and *Tango and Cash*, and on such TV shows as Fox's *Scariest Places on Earth*. A visit to the Mansfield reformatory was included in the Travel Channel's list of "101 Things to Do Before You Die."

The **Ohio State Reformatory Historic Site** (100 Reformatory Rd., Mansfield; 419-522-2644) is now open for tours (including *The Dungeon Tour* and *The Hollywood Tour*) on Sundays starting the week after Mother's Day through the end of September. Some of the guides are former guards, and the visitors have included former inmates who have returned, sometimes with family, to look at the place where they spent a chunk of their lives. The tour includes places where the movies were shot. Guides point out that Gates Brown, a baseball player with the Detroit Tigers, served a term here for burglary in the 1950s, and Cleveland Browns star running back Kevin Mack once spent a month here on a drug charge.

The Mansfield Reformatory Gift Shop sells movie memorabilia, hats, T-shirts, and keychains, and also some crafts made by present-day prisoners down the road at the new prison.

HANG ON SLOOPY

State legislators perpetrated an act of musical silliness in 1985 when they decided we had to have an official "state rock song."

The song they chose was "Hang On Sloopy," written by Celina native Rick Derringer. It was first recorded by a Dayton rock band, the McCoys, in 1965.

House Concurrent Resolution No. 16 makes you wonder just how much useful business got done in the state legislature back in the 1980s. Just read a bit of the legislation passed to create the state rock song:

"WHEREAS, the members of the 116th General Assembly of Ohio wish to recognize the rock song "Hang On Sloopy" as the official rock song of the great state of Ohio, and

"WHEREAS, if fans of jazz, country-and-western, classical, Hawaiian, and polka music think those styles also should be recognized by the state, then by golly, they can push their own resolution just like we're doing.

"WHEREAS, "Hang On Sloopy" is of particular relevance to members of the Baby Boom Generation, who were once dismissed as a bunch of long-haired, crazy kids, but who now are old enough and vote in sufficient numbers to be taken quite seriously, and

"WHEREAS, adoption of this resolution will not take too long, cost the state anything, or affect the quality of life in this state to any appreciable degree, and if we the legislature just go ahead and pass the darn thing, we can get on with more important stuff ..."

Let history note that they passed "the darn thing."

Here are the words to "Hang On Sloopy," Ohio's official rock song:

Sloopy lives in a very bad part of town,
And everybody there tries to put my Sloopy down.
Sloopy, I don't care what your daddy do.
'Cause you know Sloopy girl, I'm in love with you.
And so I'm singin'

Chorus:
Hang on Sloopy, Sloopy hang on.
Hang on Sloopy, Sloopy hang on.

Sloopy let your hair down girl, let it hang down on me.
Sloopy let your hair down girl, let it hang down on me.
Come on Sloopy Come on, Come on Sloopy come on.
Well come on Sloopy come on, come on, Sloopy come on.
Well it feels so good Come on, come on.
You know it feels so good come on, come on.
Well shake it, shake it, shake it, Sloopy Come on, come on.
Well shake it, shake it, shake it yeah.
Yeah …

[Chorus]

Yeah, yeah, yeah, yeah …

Doesn't that just have "Ohio" written all over it?

One of Johnny Appleseed's Original Trees
MANSFIELD

This place is a real mixed bag. It's perhaps the oldest veterans meeting hall in the country. It's a former zoo. It's an unusual museum. And it's haunted.

The **Mansfield Memorial Museum** (34 Park Ave. W., Mansfield; 419-525-2491) opened its doors back in 1889. Veterans who fought at Gettysburg and Shiloh met in these rooms, as did those who charged up San Juan Hill during the Spanish-American War. Next came the vets who fought in France in World War I, and so on. Now veterans of Vietnam and the Gulf War use the same chairs that Civil War veterans did to hold their meetings.

The building was also the first zoo in Mansfield. They kept live exotic animals, like monkeys and rheas, in cages on the third floor. The

This family of deceased ducks dresses for dinner in their cozy glass case at the Mansfield Memorial Museum.

zoo closed when the animals died, so they mounted them—and you can still see some of them today.

As for the ghost, the present curator reports that he has heard footsteps on the upper floors, and he says that when he displayed a picture of the first curator (whom he believes to be the ghost) the subject was frowning, but when he came back the next day, the man appeared to be smiling.

The museum was reopened a few years ago with the original 1889 display cases and a wild and wonderful collection befitting a museum from the Gay '90s.

Besides uniforms and swords from all the wars mentioned above there are the collections of stuffed birds (some now extinct), fish, and butterflies; native American artifacts; pieces of wood from Oliver Hazard Perry's flagship the *Lawrence*; a handmade pike used by John Brown in his Harpers Ferry raid; and a Victorian assembly of stuffed animals dressed up in clothes and shown taking part in human activities. They even have an apple tree that was originally planted by the legendary Johnny Appleseed. The whole tree!

Open weekends, and by appointment at other times.

A Sundae with Everything—Including the Kitchen Sink

MEDINA

Ohio has two ice-cream museums. One is operated by the Velvet Ice Cream Company in Utica.

The other is in Medina, at Elm Farms, once one of the larger dairies in northern Ohio.

Carl Abell had actually been out of the business for a few years when he started making ice cream again to go along with an ice-cream museum he installed in his former dairy.

What makes his operation unusual is a sundae that they serve called "The Kitchen Sink." It's literally served in a stainless-steel sink. The sundae, which costs in the neighborhood of $40, contains at least 21 dips of different premium ice-cream flavors, topped with a rainbow of syrups, toppings, and whipped cream.

Unlike some of the other giant-size servings offered by promotion-minded restaurateurs, this one you pay for even if you manage to eat the whole thing.

The Elm Farms Dairy and Once Upon a Sundae Ice Cream Parlor are located at 1050 West Lafayette Road, Medina; 330-722-3839.

The Inventor of the Electric Chair

MILAN

Thomas Edison, not wanting himself associated with capital punishment, went to great lengths to make sure the world's first electric chair was powered by his biggest competitor, George Westinghouse.

Another Ohioan, Dr. Alphonso David Rockwell (who also hailed from Edison's hometown of Milan) was a more willing participant.

Rockwell was noted for his research into medical uses for electricity and was selected for a committee of five persons directed to design and build the world's first electric chair for Auburn Prison in New York. He seemed to relish the challenge, and he drew up the plans for the first chair, which took the life of convicted murderer William Kemmler, alias John Hart, on August 6, 1890. He also wrote about it in his autobiography, *Rambling Recollection*, which was published in 1920. (Edison didn't even mention the chair in his own book.)

The Day the Sky Fell
NEW CONCORD

On May 1, 1860, the folks in New Concord must have thought the sky was really falling.

Residents reported hearing a humongous roar that lasted nearly a minute. It was near high noon on a clear day, and across the heavens a meteorite had entered the earth's atmosphere and was headed straight for the tiny community. As it hit the dense atmosphere it started breaking up, leaving a trail of fireworks across the sky and in all likelihood frightening the bejesus out of people and animals.

The only casualty occurred when one piece of the meteorite slammed into a cow, killing it instantly. Folks all over the county were later picking up bits of the meteorite—more than 500 pounds of space rock in all (and scientists say they probably missed much more that buried itself in the ground of Muskingum County). One of the largest chunks of meteorite recovered weighed more than 100 pounds; it is now owned by the geology department of Marietta College.

The only casualty occurred when one piece of the meteorite slammed into a cow.

The Last Sword Maker in America

NEW LONDON

It's no secret why swords don't sell all that well anymore. They haven't been used in battle since the Civil War. There just isn't much demand now for a four-foot blade.

But in New London, tiny **Ames Sword Company** (S. Railroad St.; 800-345-3682) keeps the sword-making tradition alive.

The company started out in 1791 in Chelmsford, Massachusetts. In 1832 they signed their first contract with the U.S. government to make swords for artillerymen. After that, Ames swords were carried in just about every famous military battle that the U.S. fought. Privates and presidents have carried and owned Ames swords. The first presentation swords ever commissioned by the government, to honor heroes of the Mexican War in the early 1800s, were made by Ames.

The business was sold during the Great Depression to a Columbus firm, and again in 1951 to C. E. Ward Company of New London.

Surprisingly, swords are still made much as they were two hundred years ago, one at a time, by hand. Who buys them? Fraternal organizations, like the Masons and Knights of Columbus, account for a large portion of the number made each year. The U.S. armed forces still use them for ceremonial purposes.

Sadly, after I mentioned this company in one of my books, they were inundated by people who wanted to take tours of the factory. There had been a longstanding, informal understanding that if someone dropped in at the factory and wanted to look around, and an employee could be found who was not too busy, a tour would quickly be arranged. That came to a screeching halt when they started spending a good part of the day doing tours and not getting any work done. You're still invited to stop in at the factory and browse through their store, where you can see samples of the various swords they sell. (You are invited to buy a sword, too, if you are in the market.) But don't ask for a tour. They say they are just too busy. You can take a virtual tour at their website (www.amessword.com).

Ride Till You Hurl: The New Philadelphia Carousel

NEW PHILADELPHIA

There's a graceful 36-seat, all-wood antique carousel in New Philadelphia that local families have ridden for four or five generations. And there's something special about this particular carousel. The operators let you ride till you almost toss your cookies.

This may be the longest carousel ride in existence. They don't use a timer and just let the thing go, round and round, until the operator notices a kid getting a bit green or starting to look frantically around for Mom or Dad. To be honest, that really doesn't happen so often. Most kids love it. It's like getting on the ride and having the operator forget you're on board.

Here's the next good part. The cost of the ride is just 50 cents.

The Herschell-Spillman carousel, built in 1928 in North Tonawanda, New York, was purchased second hand in 1940 by the city fathers of New Philadelphia. They wanted a special attraction for **Tuscora Park** (161 Tuscora Ave., New Philadelphia; 330-343-6814), the city playground. Today there are a half-dozen other kiddy rides, as well as a Ferris wheel, a huge swimming pool, and a youth center.

They just let the thing go round and round until the operator notices a kid getting a bit green.

Sasquatch Hunter

NEWCOMERSTOWN

Don Keating of Newcomerstown has devoted about half of his life to research on sightings of Sasquatch, or "Bigfoot."

Although Sasquatch is best known through sightings in the northwestern U.S., Don says there have been sightings in nearly every state in the union.

In Ohio alone, there have been more than 200 sightings in the last two decades.

Keating himself has never seen a real Sasquatch, but, he quickly adds, that doesn't mean they don't exist.

The reason he says this is a set of plaster casts he made 10 years ago along a lonely road in Tuscarawas County.

It was about 1990 that Don received word of a Bigfoot sighting along Big Lick Road, just outside of Newcomerstown. He went to the area and searched for evidence but found nothing. Over the next year he occasionally checked out the same area, and one day as he was driving down the road he spotted something unusual.

On a muddy stretch alongside the road he spotted three huge, widely spaced, footprints. Each footprint was 17 inches long and nearly 11 inches wide at the toe spread. Their depth in the mud seemed to indicate a very heavy animal or object, one that weighed six to eight hundred pounds. Also judging by the spread of the footprints, they would have to have been made by something with a stride of four to six feet.

Keating made plaster casts of what he found and has shown them to hunters and other outdoors experts, but no one so far has been able to pinpoint what could have made such large and widely spaced footprints. Keating also points out that there had been no publicity, and no one knew that he periodically checked the area, so he rules out some kind of hoax.

What did he find? Keating still isn't sure, but he doesn't rule out the footprints of an Ohio Sasquatch. He holds annual meetings in Newcomerstown for other researchers into Sasquatch phenomena.

Harry Stevens and the Hot Dog

NILES

The next time you hear the phrase "As American as baseball, hot dogs, apple pie, and ice cream," think of Harry Stevens. The Niles native created the American hot dog as we know it today.

Stevens operated concessions at several big sporting complexes around the turn of the 20th century. He sold things like scorecards, hard-boiled eggs, beer, and popcorn at games.

One very cold day in 1901 at a New York Giants game at the old polo grounds, ice cream and cold beer were just not selling. Harry had an inspiration. He sent his workers into the surrounding neighborhood to buy out all the little sausages, called "dachshund sausages," and Vienna rolls. Back at the ball yard they quickly boiled the sausages in a large vat of water, sliced open the rolls, plunked the puffed-up wieners between the bread halves, and slathered on some mustard. Then, for the first time in history, fans heard the cry, "Get yer redhots here! Get 'em while they're hot!"

The hot sandwiches were an instant hit.

In the crowd that fateful day was sports cartoonist Thomas Aloysius Dorgan. He noticed the new sandwich being sold and drew a cartoon. It featured four-legged frankfurters and the patrons reaching for them. Dorgan couldn't remember how to spell "dachshund," so in the caption he just wrote "Hot Dog." The rest, as they say, is history.

Stevens never forgot his Ohio roots. Despite his successes in the concessions biz, he and his wife Mary and their kids always lived in Niles, and today there is a city park in Niles that honors Harry Stevens, the father of the "hot dog."

This Museum Officially Sucks

NORTH CANTON

In 1910, the new Kotten suction cleaner required the user to stand on a platform and rock back and forth. The rocking action activated a bellows under the platform that created the suction to clean with. It gave the operator quite a workout and was very slow in cleaning. But considering the alternative at the time—hauling the carpet out to a clothesline and then beating it with a stick—it probably seemed like a really neat invention.

Here's an invention you can't beat with a stick!

The **Hoover Historical Center** (1875 Easton St. NW, North Canton; 330-499-0287) has the Kotton on display. Today Ohio lays claim to the only vacuum cleaner museum in the nation. Here you can also see the first cleaning machine sold by Hoover way back in 1908; it weighed almost 40 pounds! Carry that one up and down the stairs a few times. They also have a Hoover cleaner called a Constellation that was a big hit in the 1950s. When you turn it on, it floats on a cushion of air. There were no wheels, so it could easily follow you wherever you went.

You can also find some interesting items used by housewives years before suction cleaners were invented.

A New Use for Covered Bridges

NORTH KINGSVILLE

What do you do with a covered bridge you no longer need? Ashtabula County recently put one of theirs up for sale, with the stipulation that the buyer had to move it. A local entrepreneur bought the bridge, sawed it in two, and moved one half to North Kingsville and the other to Andover . . . to become pizza restaurants. Today you can grab a cheese and pepperoni pie while gazing at the initials and graffiti carved into the timbers of the old bridge a century or more ago at the original **Covered Bridge Pizza** (6541 South Main Street, North Kingsville; 440-224-2252).

The Tracks to the Underground

OBERLIN

You're driving along Professor Street in Oberlin, and suddenly, across from the Conservatory of Music, you see a strange sight: a pair of railroad tracks rising into the air. It looks like the tracks sprouted from some collapsed underground railroad. The first time I saw it, I thought it was a college prank.

Turns out, it's a piece of outdoor sculpture and a symbol of the role Oberlin and Oberlin College played in the Underground Railroad before the Civil War.

Oberlin was a strong abolitionist community, firmly against slavery. In fact, it has been called "the little town that started the Civil War." The Underground Railroad was a series of homes and buildings across the northern states during the early 19th century that sheltered escaped slaves and helped them make their way to freedom in Canada.

In 1977, Oberlin College architectural student Cameron Armstrong, class of '77, designed the railroad tracks coming out of the ground. It was only meant to be a temporary project, but its popularity has made it a permanent fixture. You can see it today in front of Talcott Hall on South Professor Street near the intersection of West College Street.

World's Largest Crayon
SANDUSKY

May 28, 1997 must have been a glorious day for the Dixon Ticonderoga Company. That's when their Sandusky production facility turned out the world's largest crayon.

The company alternately hails it as "The World's Largest Soybean Crayon," which seems a bit redundant if it's already the world's largest crayon, period. But it's their claim to fame, so I guess they can claim it however they want. Anyway, it's in the *Guiness Book of World Records*.

Made as a publicity stunt to promote the the company's new Prang soybean crayons, it weighed 330 pounds and measured 10 feet long. It took 55 gallons of soybean oil to make it—that's about a quarter of an acre of soybean crop (enough to produce 34,527 ordinary crayons). It was red.

Note the use of the past tense in this description. Despite the crayon's record-setting size, the company seems to have misplaced it.

The Giants of Seville
SEVILLE

Once, giants walked among us. At least they did in the Medina County farming village of Seville.

In the Mound Hill Cemetery in Seville, there is a tall stone statue of a woman. Some say it is supposed to be a likeness of Anna Swan Bates. It stands over the graves of Anna and her husband, Martin Bates, once known worldwide as the "World's Tallest Married Couple."

Bates, who stood just a hair under eight feet tall, had been a Confederate soldier in the Civil War. His wife, Anna Swan Bates, who was about an inch or two taller than her husband, was born in Nova Scotia and had been discovered by P. T. Barnum. The two met when Bates went to work for Barnum after the Civil War, and they eventually married. They toured the world, appearing before the crowned heads of Europe.

A couple of circus friends happened to own farms in Seville, and

Captain Martin Bates (above) was one half of the world's tallest married couple when he was married to Anna Swan Bates.

during the off-season the Bateses visited their friends and enjoyed the small town and its rural countryside so much they also decided to buy a farm and make Seville their home.

It was while living in Seville that Anna Bates became pregnant and, after a difficult delivery on January 18, 1879, gave birth to a giant baby boy—30 inches long and 23 1/2 pounds at birth. Each of his feet was six inches long. Sadly, he only lived 11 hours. He, too, is buried in the Mound Hill Cemetery.

Captain Bates had his farm home custom built. The ceilings were 14 feet high, all the doors were 8 1/2 feet tall, even the cellar was more than 9 feet deep. The specially built furniture was so massive that when average-sized guests visited, the women would usually stand rather than suffer the indignity of having to be hoisted up onto the seat. In those pre-automobile days, the Bateses had a specially built carriage that was pulled by two giant Clydesdale workhorses. After being forced to stand during a service at the local Baptist church because they were too tall to fit in the regular-sized church pews, Bates had a special large pew made just for his family, so they could sit during the service.

On August 5 of 1888, Anna Swan Bates died of kidney failure. She was just 42 years old. Captain Bates telegraphed a casket company in Cleveland to send a casket to hold the remains of a person eight feet tall. The casket company, thinking the size was a misprint, sent a normal-sized casket. Bates went into a fury over the mistake, and they had to delay the funeral three days until the special casket could be constructed and shipped to Seville.

Following his wife's funeral, Bates, taking no chances on a repeat of the casket fiasco, ordered a second extra-long casket for himself and stored it in his barn for years until it was finally needed.

Bates was lonely after the death of Anna and a few years later married Annette Weatherby, the five-foot-tall daughter of his pastor. He also gave up the giant house on the farm and moved into a normal-sized home in downtown Seville. (He did enlarge the bedroom to hold his 10-foot-long bed, and he brought with him some of his favorite chairs.)

From all accounts the tall captain had a short temper, and old age did not improve his disposition. He took to chewing tobacco in his later years and was known to spit at people he did not like. His investments and the income from his farm allowed him to live out his life comfortably in the little northern Ohio town. He died at the age of 74 in January of 1919.

A few old-timers in Seville still remember Captain Bates. Many of the places associated with his life still stand. The **Seville Historical Society** (70 W. Main St., Seville; 330-769-4056) has some of his clothing and life-size pictures of him and his first wife, Anna Swan Bates, that visitors can pose with. The farm home is gone, but the barn still remains.

In the Mound Hill Cemetery, the statue to Anna Bates now stands eternal guard over the graves of Martin, Anna, and their baby.

Lions and Tigers and Bears and Bed and Breakfast

SUGARCREEK

The **Bed and Breakfast Barn** (560 Sugarcreek St., Sugarcreek; 330-852-2337) is a rustic country inn with the usual amenities—and a basement full of animals.

The basement contains the White Fawn Wildlife Exhibit—more than 300 mounted animals ranging from cougars to deer to a host of other North American wildlife. You can see black bears stalking trout, wild turkeys about to take flight at the approach of mountain

lions, and many other animals, all mounted in settings that make them look almost like they did in life. You don't even have to spend the night at the bed and breakfast. For $1 per person they offer tours of the exhibit to anyone who drops in.

Now before you get excited and start writing letters, Tom Agler, the owner, didn't kill any of these animals. He purchased them from collectors and at disposal sales held by law-enforcement organizations that had confiscated them originally from poachers and other individuals who had obtained them illegally.

If you prefer your animals alive, the Bed and Breakfast Barn also has a petting zoo with deer, goats, donkeys, llamas, rabbits, chickens, ducks, and two bears.

The Budget

SUGARCREEK

"Joseph Yoder had a big explosion, but it turned out to just be a strawberry can. It flew all the way up to the ceiling and made quite a mess."

That's the kind of news story you're likely to read in *The Budget*, the small Sugarcreek newspaper published for Amish and Mennonite readers locally and throughout the world.

The reporters, or "scribes," as they are called, are members of the Amish and Mennonite communities, and their "stories" are in the form of long letters that they write to the editor of the newspaper, who then publishes them pretty much as they are written.

It may seem quaint to some, but *The Budget* sells big time, not only to the Amish and Mennonites, but also to many other people around the world who enjoy reading about the simple lifestyle of the "plain people," and enjoy the sometimes unintentional humor of their writing: "Dennis Miller started out to plow this morning and came across a soft place when all at once the horse went down and all that would have been needed would be a few shovels of dirt and he would have been covered up."

Then there's the way they can often look on the bright side, even when reporting a serious accident: "David L. Yoder had quite an experience late Monday, when he got gas on his clothes, which caught fire. He buried himself in hay and smothered the flames. It is a great wonder that the hay didn't start to burn. He got a few burns on his neck and lost some hair and whiskers, but his clothes aren't damaged much."

The Budget is now in its second century, and little has changed since it began publication in 1890.

The Sign of the Three Crosses

SUGARCREEK

If you travel rural Ohio you may have seen them. Three crosses: two blue and one yellow. No signs, no banners, just three simple wooden crosses, usually standing beside a rural road.

The man responsible for them was Bernie Coffindaffer. A self-made millionaire from West Virginia, Coffindaffer was told by Jesus, in a 1983 vision, to go around the country putting up the crosses. And Jesus told him just what the crosses should look like.

Coffindaffer sold his business and spent the rest of his life finding locations, getting permission, and building crosses. By 1993, when he died, he had 1,800 sets of three crosses in 29 states and in the Philippines. Friends said that he spent over three million dollars in his pilgrimage, all of his savings, to complete his mission.

There are 89 locations in Ohio where Bernie Coffindaffer placed crosses. But now, years after his death, maintenance on most of the crosses has ceased. Some have fallen down or been taken down by property owners. In a few cases they have been kept standing as a silent tribute to one man's faith in his God.

One set of crosses in particularly good condition is on Ohio Route 39, on the east side of Sugarcreek.

World's Largest Gathering of Twins

TWINSBURG

Would the world's largest gathering of twins be as exciting in a town called Millsville? Probably not. Luckily, Moses and Aaron Wilcox had their way back in 1819.

When the twin Wilcox brothers moved to what was then known as Millsville, they didn't like the name and offered the tiny community six acres of the land they were clearing for a public square in the village, and $20 toward the start of a school, if the community would agree to change the name to Twinsburg.

The townspeople complied but didn't decide to celebrate the name until a festival honoring twins was first organized in 1976.

Only 37 sets of twins, mostly from northern Ohio, showed up for that first one-day event. They spent the day dedicating a monument to the Wilcox brothers and partaking in the usual small-town festival events.

They had so much fun, they repeated the festival the next year, and every year since.

Over the years, **Twins Days** (330-425-3652) has grown from a little local gathering into a two-day international festival attracting nearly 3,000 sets of twins each year from as far away as Poland and Nigeria. (Other "multiples"—triplets, quads, and even quintuplets—participate.) Today the festival draws coverage from news media all over the world. The last year I covered the festival I spotted TV crews from Japan, England, and Germany. By 1993 the budget was topping $200,000 a year, and the city was hiring professional promoters to stage the event. It is held the first full weekend in August.

The festival is now listed in the *Guinness Book of World Records* as the largest gathering of twins in the world. They have featured a double wedding of two sets of twins, and efforts are underway to build a Twins Hall of Fame in the community.

The Town Where They Race Worms
VERMILION

Vermilion, Ohio, may be the only place on earth where thousands of people come together each autumn to watch worms race.

The event was conceived of by Dick Goddard, one of the most widely respected and admired weathermen in the U.S. (and a colleague of mine at FOX 8 TV). Dick has had a long love affair with bugs, birds, and animals. He hugs them all. For example, a spider once crawled down a web onto my desk in the newsroom. Startled, I knocked the spider to the floor and was about to dispatch it by stepping on it when Goddard stopped me, carefully scooped it up in a plastic cup, and then carried it outside to release it. That's the kind of guy he is. So it came as no surprise when he told me his longtime ambition to sponsor or conduct a festival for the woollybear caterpillar.

Woollybears are those little furry worms we see in late summer and early fall. They have fuzzy coats of brown and orange. Weather folklore claims that the severity of the coming winter can be predicted by the woollybear caterpillars' fuzzy coats—something about the length of the brown part, or it is the orange? (I sometimes think Goddard makes it up as he goes along.)

The Woollybear Festival started as a PTA fundraiser in Birmingham and has grown over more than 20 years into the largest single-day festival in Ohio, attracting upwards of 150,000 people to the small town of Vermilion (where it was moved after the first couple of years to better accommodate the crowd).

The worm races are the highlight of the festival. Ever seen a worm race? It's about as exciting as watching paint dry on a wall. Nevertheless people pack this small town to watch the races, and to dress up their children (and dogs, cats, and pot-bellied pigs) as worms.

The annual Woollybear Festival is held in Vermilion in late September or early October each year (depending on the Cleveland Browns schedule—Goddard is team statistician at home games). Call the Vermilion Chamber of Commerce (440-967-3467) for the date of this year's festival.

OHIO'S BIRTHDAY—
MARCH OR AUGUST?

**The history books tell us that Ohio became a state—
the first state carved out of the old Northwest
Territory—on March 1, 1803.
But that's not entirely correct.**

The U.S. Congress never got around to formally voting on the resolution admitting Ohio to the Union until August. Of 1953.

Proponents of Ohio statehood had done a lot of lobbying in Washington, and in 1802 Congress did indeed pass the enabling bill that authorized the formation of a state government in Ohio. Citizens held a constitutional convention in Chillicothe and started sending representatives and senators to Washington. But in all the excitement Congress forgot to vote on accepting us as a new state. They didn't get around to it for 150 years.

Now some historians say it was just a formality and didn't mean anything. Nevertheless, in 1953 with a few smiles and snickers, President Dwight Eisenhower signed the resolution into law, saying he wanted Ohioans to "legally" celebrate their 150th birthday.

A Springfield, Ohio, Congressman, Clarence Brown, had jokingly threatened to apply for foreign aid for Ohio if the resolution did not pass Congress this time.

But some Americans in other states didn't find it very humorous. They pointed to the number of Ohioans who had served, apparently illegitimately, as president of the United States, not to mention the countless laws and bills that had been pushed through Congress by our illegally seated representatives and senators.

The president of a Georgia college even went so far as to file a federal suit in 1984 to stop Ohioans from voting in the elections that year, claiming the 1953 action by Congress was unconstitutional. He lost the suit.

So Happy Birthday, Ohio, either on March 1, 1803, or August 7, 1953.

A Letter on a Grain of Rice

WALNUT CREEK

"The Lord is my shepherd, I shall not want, he maketh me to lie down in green pastures." Deborah Kramer once wrote that excerpt from Psalm 23 on a single grain of rice.

Deborah had been doing calligraphy since she was a child, and after she and her husband, Stephen, heard about rice writing, she decided to give that a try.

Rice writing dates back two thousand years. In Turkey, a man once wrote two hundred letters on a single grain of rice. It's on exhibit in a museum in Topkapi Palace in Istanbul.

Deborah does the rice writing with a very fine pen, with a point about the size of a piece of hair. She works using a video camera with close-up lens that enlarges what she is working on and projects it on a nearby 21-inch TV. But Deborah doesn't really need the magnification, she just writes with a firm, steady hand, never even looking at the TV.

You can find Deborah and Stephen writing on rice and making jewelry from their finished product at the **Holmes County Amish Flea Market** (3149 State Rte. 39, Walnut Creek; 330-893-2836) every Thursday, Friday, and Saturday.

The Center of the World

WARREN

 Ohio is the center of the world. If you don't believe it, just ask the Ohio Department of Transportation. They put up one of their familiar green-and-white reflecting signs proclaiming the fact. The precise "Center of the World," according to ODOT, is along a sparsely populated stretch of State Route 5, just outside of Warren.

This designation got its start in the 1840s when Randell Wilmot moved to the area from Pennsylvania. He opened up a store, stagecoach stop, bar, and lunch stand and called the complex "The Center of the World." For lonely travelers in the 1840s, the title was probably appropriate.

However, when the Cleveland and Mahoning Railroad started taking away much of his business, Wilmot closed up the Center of the World and moved east to Cortland, Ohio. There he began another business, which he called "The End of the World." That proved to be prophetic, at least for Wilmot; he died in Cortland.

SauerKraut Festival

WAYNESVILLE

It has been reported in national publications that Ohio has more festivals than any other state. That's probably true. Pick any county, town, or village—sometime during the year they're sure to be celebrating something. Everything from flowers (the Carnation Festival in Alliance) to worms (the Woollybear Festival in Vermilion—see "The Town Where They Race Worms").

There's the Melon Festival in Milan, the Strawberry Festival in Norwalk, and the Grape Festival in Geneva. How about the Covered Bridge Festival in Ashtabula, and the Festival of the Fish in Vermilion? There are also the potato festivals in Mantua and in Amherst.

Now, in most cases the reason for the festival is obvious: they raise a lot of the honored fruit or vegetables in that area, or are known for a great number of covered bridges. But that's not always so.

Take Waynesville, for instance. Waynesville is known as the Antique Capital of the Midwest. It must be true—*USA Today* said so several years ago, and no other city complained or filed a counterclaim. So the chamber of commerce in Waynesville adopted the title. Naturally, you'd expect a town with such a well-established claim to fame to host an antique festival. Nope. They do sauerkraut.

Why sauerkraut? They must raise a lot of cabbage around here. Nope again. Okay, a lot of German or Bavarian immigrants settled here, right? Nope. Perhaps a more obscure connection to sauerkraut? Nope.

Back in 1970 (long before the antiques title took hold), a meeting was held among local merchants trying to stir up interest in a sidewalk sale they held each autumn.

One merchant belched and said, "Excuse me, I had some really good sauerkraut for lunch." His comment was like divine intervention. "Mmm. I like sauerkraut, too," said another merchant. Several others added their endorsement of fermented cabbage as one of life's nobler pleasures. And then it happened. One of the merchants shouted out, "Let's sponsor a sauerkraut dinner!"

They did, and it was so successful that the dinner grew into an annual festival, each year's event getting bigger and better until now a quarter of a million people swamp this tiny village each October to tramp past crafts booths and booths selling food—including sauerkraut candy and even ice cream. (I've tried the candy, not bad.)

Check with the Waynesville Chamber of Commerce (513-897-8855) for festival dates.

A Victorian ATM
WELLINGTON

Most of us have used an automated teller machine. But how many of us know that the device was pioneered by an Ohio bank? In early 1970, the world's first "money machine" was installed at the City National Bank on Tremont Road in Columbus.

Now, before you start writing to tell me that *your* bank was the first to install an ATM, note this: no less an authority than the Smithsonian Institution in Washington, D.C., asked to enshrine the Columbus machine. (The Smithsonian didn't wind up with it; City National had been bought up by another bank that either couldn't find the original ATM or didn't want to donate it.)

There is another notable ATM currently on display in Ohio, though. The **LorMet Community Federal Credit Union** (216 N. Main St., Wellington; 440-647-1999) has a money machine shaped like a horse and carriage. Yep, a life-size fiberglass horse pulling a Victorian carriage. (The ATM is located inside the carriage.)

LorMet officials say it was the idea of their CEO, Daniel Cwalina, who wanted the modern ATM to blend in with the Victorian charm of downtown Wellington. The horse, they say, was easy to find, but a carriage that would fit over an ATM vault was another matter. They finally had to have a custom-made buggy that reaches all the way to the ground.

The display was so realistic that at first some customers thought it was just one of the many area Amish families doing a little banking.

Today, most everyone has caught on.

Komar the Magnificent!
Komar the Cheesemaker!
WILMOT

Most folks who walked into Alpine-Alpa, a Wilmot tourist spot that combines a cheese shop and a Swiss-style restaurant, never knew that the short, balding, bewhiskered man behind the counter for 50 years had a strange secret.

Vernon Craig, mild-mannered shopkeeper, needs but a straw hat and a pair of broad-fall jeans to blend right in with his Amish neighbors. But Vernon has an alter ego. He travels the world and appears on television, in magazines, and newspapers . . . as "The Amazing Komar."

This former cheesemaker holds a permanent Guinness world record for the longest fire walk in his bare feet—more than 25 feet.

He also has held Guinness titles for the longest time lying on a bed of nails and the "most weight borne while lying on a bed of nails."

Vernon didn't set out to be an entertainer. Back in 1969 he was a tireless advocate for the mentally retarded. But at one point, concerned that people were listening but not hearing his message, he decided to try to get people's attention a different way—by lying down on a bed of nails.

The stunt got their attention all right. He had never tried anything like it before, and he made the bed of nails himself. When he dropped onto the nails, the tips dug into his back, and he left a trail of blood when he got up.

Needless to say, a show like that brought him a lot of attention. He was soon invited to appear at other gatherings. (As he went along he learned how to control the pain.) By the age of 69, he had appeared in more than 100 countries on six continents. He set the world record for his fire walk in England when he strolled barefoot through 25 feet of burning coals at a temperature of 1,494°F. He has appeared on several major network TV shows in the U.S. and also on television in other parts of the world. *The Guinness Book of World Records* honored him with statues in several of their museums (the closest is in Niagara Falls, Canada).

New ownership of the Alpine Alpa forced Komar into semiretirement, but recently he put on the old fakir costume for a special event. As he arose from the bed of nails, there were puncture wounds but very little blood—and within moments the holes on his back had disappeared. How does he do it? Komar says it's all a matter of controlling your mind.

World's Largest Cuckoo Clock

WILMOT

Alice Grossniklaus, shrewd businesswoman and amateur yodeler, wanted to draw attention to her cheese shop and restaurant. Recalling the popularity of cuckoo clocks in her native Switzerland, she decided to build one here in Wilmot. While she was at it, she decided to make it the biggest cuckoo clock ever.

According to the *Guinness Book of World Records*, she succeeded. And now, thanks to Alpine-Alpa Restaurant, little Wilmot, Ohio, lays claim to being the "Cuckoo Clock Capital of America."

It took Grossniklaus 12 years, from 1962 to 1974. She imported the nine half-life-size carved wooden figures, which dance and play together in an oom-pah band on the hour and half hour, and had a local Amish craftsman build the clock. The chiming giant is 23 1/2 feet high, 24 feet wide, and 13 1/2 feet deep.

There is no charge to visit and watch the clock strike every 30 minutes.

Other states have claimed larger cuckoos, but those have been buildings altered to look like clocks. This one is a true, working, stand-alone clock.

The clock is open to the public spring through fall at **Alpine-Alpa Restaurant** (1504 U.S. Rte. 62, Wilmot; 330-359-5454).

One Big Madonna

WINDSOR

If you like your religious symbols big, I mean really big, it's hard to beat the 50-foot-tall Our Lady of Guadaloupe in Windsor.

How this statue came to rise above a rural Ohio farm is a story of faith and determination. Pat and Ed Heinz bought the 50-acre farm in 1987, but three years later when some investments went bad, the Heinzes lost the farm in bankruptcy proceedings. They moved to England so Ed could pursue work in nuclear engineering, but within just a few years they were able to move back and buy the farm again.

They decided to dedicate the farm to God and formed the **Servants of Mary Center for Peace** (6569 Ireland Rd., Windsor; 440-272-5380). They were moved to construct a statue to Our Lady of Guadaloupe alongside a small lake in the middle of the farm. It was supposed to

be 30 feet high, but by the time it was completed it topped out at more than 50 feet. A lighted 1,150-foot-long illuminated rosary rings the lake in front of the statue.

The Heinzes are devout Catholics, but they say their center is open to all religions. There is a meeting hall and gift shop, and there are other shrines on the property.

SOUTHEAST

The Sign of the Cow
BARNESVILLE

Anyone who has lived on a farm knows what "the sign of the cow" is. You might unexpectedly step in it while crossing the pasture. But near Barnesville, on the south side of I-70, there is a different kind of cow sign that's a bit more interesting. It's a billboard shaped like a longhorn cow. Its owners claim it is the world's largest wooden longhorn cow.

Okay.

The cow sign is 28 feet high and 64 feet long from its tail to the tips of its longhorns. It was built by the Dickinson Cattle Company, which may well have the largest longhorn cattle ranch in Ohio.

They had a little problem with the tail. There was a lot of wind at the top of the hill, so they knew the slender 12-foot-long tail had to be reinforced, but with what? If they need guy wires, the cattle grazing around the sign would probably stretch the wires by using them to scratch against. Sheets of steel proved to be too heavy for the sign. Then someone had a simple idea: why not let the tail swing free, like a real cow's tail? A hinge at the top of the tail solved the problem, and now truckers driving by the huge sign on a windy night might swear the giant silhouette of a longhorn steer comes to life when its tail starts to sway in the breeze.

Last of the Mail Pouch Barn Painters
BELMONT

Harley Warrick was a barn painter. If you have traveled through Ohio, you have seen his work—the barns with the fading signs that say "Chew Mail Pouch Tobacco, Treat Yourself to the Best."

In fact, Harley was the last of the Mail Pouch barn painters.

A resident of Belmont, Harley painted the Mail Pouch message on the side of an estimated 22,000 barns in Ohio and nine other states.

The painting of advertisements on barns had been going on for over a century. Right after World War II, Harley, just back from fighting in Europe, had developed a wanderlust and didn't want to go back to the farm. One day the Mail Pouch painters came to paint his father's barn. He spent the afternoon talking with and watching the men and decided that this was something he could do. When they left that day, he went with them and began a career that spanned nearly half a century. As Harley put it, "I'd seen some things in Europe, I wanted to see some things here."

In the first 20 years he would paint as many as two to three barns a day, six days a week!

Watching Harley at work in his last years was watching a master at his craft. Harley would clean away the weeds from around the bottom of whichever side of the barn he was going to paint. He would puff on his pipe as he silently calculated how much paint to mix and where to hang his scaffolding and place his ladders.

When he started painting, it was with quick, sure, even strokes. The message started popping out of the paint as he progressed across the face of the barn. It took him from two to three hours to complete a barn.

In 1970, Mail Pouch discontinued its painting operations and Harley started out on a freelance basis, picking and choosing the barns he wanted to paint, when he wanted to paint them. By then barns with advertisements had acquired a nostalgic value, and some owners actually paid Harley to put the sign on their barn. He was even asked once to paint the Mail Pouch message on the bottom of a swimming pool. Some of his work is now in the Smithsonian Institution. It was the best of times for the painter from Belmont, who by this time was the last person in his trade.

Harley died in 2000. He was still painting, but now it was on the sides of bird feeders shaped like miniature barns that he produced in his garage to sell to the nostalgic.

In our last meeting, some years before, I had watched him lay out his letters without any measuring or sketching, just by eyeballing the side of the barn, and leave behind a perfect blend of colors and letters. I admired his work and said "Harley, you're not a painter, you're an artist." He looked at the just-completed barn and said, "Nah, I'm just a barn-dauber."

So as you travel throughout the Midwest, if you see a fading Mail Pouch sign on the side of a barn, remember the "barn-dauber" from Belmont, Harley Warrick.

Ohio's Serengeti

CUMBERLAND

It's almost like Jurassic Park. Nearly 10,000 acres of rolling hills, valleys, and lakes are enclosed by tall, electrified security fences—to keep the beasts inside.

The Wilds (14000 International Rd., Cumberland; 740-638-5030) is a conservation, education, and science center that is home to 25 species of wildlife from Africa, Asia, and North America. Some of the animals kept here have already become extinct in the wild, and this is one of the last chances for survival of these breeds.

Located on some formerly strip-mined land once owned by utility companies, the Wilds collaborates with zoos and other wildlife conservation groups on breeding and research programs. It is open to visitors May through October. The animals range free within the enclosure; people are restricted to special buses that travel the roads.

Museum of Matchsticks
FLY

In southern Ohio, near the town of Fly, is a small museum dedicated to the life's work of a man who let a hobby get out of hand.

Jack Dempsey Johnson was a heavy-equipment operator. When medical problems caused him to retire in the 1960s, he, like so many people with time on their hands, looked for a hobby. What he found was matchsticks.

And it's what he did with the matchsticks over the next 30 years that he is remembered for. He started building things with them. First a small replica of an earthmover, then a train—complete with locomotive, two freight cars, and caboose. Then he started building replicas of buildings that he was familiar with, all Lilliputian-size, all made with matchsticks.

When he died in 1992, Johnson had constructed hundreds of tiny wooden works of art, including a replica of every building on his farm. By that time everyone in the neighborhood knew him as Matchstick Jack.

Today Matchstick Jack is gone, but his work lives on thanks to his family, who have opened the **Matchstick Jack Memorial Museum** (open by appointment only: State Rte. 800, Fly; 740-865-3035) to house his work.

The Last Washboard Manufacturer in the U.S.
LOGAN

Unless you spend a lot of time in an area where there is no running water, you may never have come in contact with a washboard. A washboard is a piece of corrugated steel or glass that you scrub clothes on. It beats scrubbing them on a rock down at the creek. Why scrub your clothes on a rock? People used to wear their clothes for several days, and believe me—they had to scrub them on something to get the smell out. Washboards also were used to make music, by scratching on the surface to keep time to folk songs.

Anyway, at one time there were dozens of washboard manufacturers in the country, but with the 1950s and the increasing popularity of automatic washers and dryers, there was a drastic drop in the sale of washboards. Most manufacturers saw the suds on the floor and went looking for a new business—all, that is, except the Columbus Washboard Company. They just ignored sliding sales and kept on making their washboards, one at a time, until, by 1999, they were the last washboard manufacturer in the country.

Despite the fact that the Amish still ordered a lot of washboards, there just wasn't a big enough market, and it looked like Columbus Washboard would finally have to call it quits too. Then an investor, George K. Richards, heard about the company and offered to buy it—lock, stock, and washboard. He put together an investment group and named Jacqui Barnett general manager.

She in turn has hired an all-female staff that does everything from cutting the boards to cutting the sheet-metal parts. (Jacqui says she has had male employees from time to time, but that they don't last long.) Oh, and they moved the company to Logan, south of Columbus, because that's where Jacqui lives, and she said she wasn't about to drive all the way to Columbus every day. They do still list the company name with a Columbus address. Today you can still find the **Columbus Washboard Company** (14 Gallagher Ave., Logan; 740-380-3828) makin' 'em one at a time. Visitors are welcome any time the factory is open. They will give free tours at the drop of a hat, just give them a call first.

Bottle-Feeding the Fish

MARIETTA

Marietta offers an exciting way to welcome spring. After watching the carp swim back up the Ohio River each April 15th, you can feed them—from baby bottles.

How do you bottle-feed a carp? One of the volunteers at the **Ohio River Museum** (601 Front St., Marietta; 800-860-0145) figured it out while working on the permanently docked sternwheeler-museum, the *W. P. Snyder Jr.* One day, while not terribly busy with muscum business, he found a baby bottle someone had left onboard. Recollecting how fish made sucking noises when they ate stale bread people tossed into the river, he decided to experiment. He leaned over the edge of the boat and filled the bottle with some river water. He crammed pieces of stale bread into the bottle, put the nipple back, and shook the whole mess a couple of times. Then he leaned over the edge of the boat again and offered the nipple to the fish. He suddenly found himself bottle-feeding a large three-foot-long carp.

Since then, museum staffers have picked up quite a collection of baby bottles, and they always keep a good supply of stale bread around. When tourists show up, the fish do, too. They're not dumb; when they hear footsteps they know they're going to get fed.

The carp arrive in spring, but you can try your hand at bottle-feeding them any day that the museum's open during the spring, summer, and fall.

It's Not Just a Stump–It's Public Art
MARIETTA

After a big windstorm crashed through Marietta in 1998, toppling many of the mature trees that helped win this community the designation "Tree City USA," civic leaders decided to try creating some beauty from the devastation.

They hired chainsaw artist David Ferguson, from Williamstown, West Virginia, just across the Ohio River, to do something with the taller tree stumps that were still standing.

He turned them into sculpture. A month of steady sawing resulted in seven chainsaw creations on park property around the city. One of the largest shows a Native American and an early pioneer standing back to back. Another shows an eagle reclaiming his roost. Still another is called the *Critter Tree* and shows several animals peeking out from within the wrecked tree.

Ferguson said that the idea of creating public art from big stumps is spreading. He said he was recently hired by a West Virginia city to turn two large tree trunks into art rather than chipping everything up and leaving just a hole in the ground. "This way the tree that has been a part of the community for many years can serve a new purpose, and it softens the loss of the shade that the tree provided," Ferguson said.

The Marietta/Washington County Convention and Visitors Bureau (316 Third St., Marietta; 800-288-2577) offers a map of the parks where the stump art is located.

A Really Big Muskie

MCCONNELLSVILLE

When you say "muskie," most people think of the muskellunge fish, a true fighting fish found in Ohio that grows to a length of four feet or better. Well, Ohio once was home to the largest muskie in the world—but this one wasn't a fish.

The Big Muskie was a piece of equipment—the second largest machine ever to "walk" the face of the earth.

The Big Muskie started life as a Model 4250W Bucyrus-Erie dragline. Actually, *the* model 4250W Bucyrus-Erie—it was the only one ever built. Her 220-cubic-yard bucket weighed 230 tons—empty. She was so big that she had to be constructed on the work site—it took three years—and she started working in 1969.

Owned by the Central Ohio Coal Company, a division of American Electric Power, the giant rig once removed the earth over coal veins in strip mines, allowing bulldozers and smaller vehicles to drive right into the seams of coal and extract it. The name came about because the area being worked was mostly in Muskingum County. The Big Muskie was hard to miss even when she was working hundreds of feet from the nearest roadway. She stood nearly 20 stories high and weighed 27 million pounds. The crane operator sat in a seat five stories off the ground. The bucket that dug the earth was the size of a two-story house, and the rig was as wide as an eight-lane highway! It took 13,800 volts of electricity to run her (almost enough electricity to run a small town). And she "walked"—on hydraulic legs that moved very, very slowly. (It took her days to move just a mile.)

The Big Muskie was used until 1991, when a depression in the demand for high-sulfur Ohio coal caused her to be parked and shut down—forever, as it turned out. New laws about surface mining and new technologies had bypassed the Big Muskie. Local preservation groups tried to save the rig as a sort of tourist attraction, or a monument to the coal industry, but despite their lobbying and fund-raising efforts, deadlines could not be met and demolition teams started dismantling the giant dragline in mid 1999.

Today the only thing left of the Big Muskie is the bucket. Even that alone is still quite remarkable; it's the size of an eight-lane highway and weighs over 230 tons.

After the Muskie was demolished, the bucket was hauled to a park in Morgan County owned by the electric company, on State Route 78 just east of McConnellsville, and today it sits on a hilltop as a memorial to miners who once worked this land to extract its coal.

A Really, Really Big Cross
NELSONVILLE

Walter Schwartz wanted to build a memorial to his wife, Elizabeth. He wanted something special, something that everyone in the valley where they lived would see. He settled for a cross. But not just any cross. What Walter Schwartz built was a 73-foot-tall illuminated cross atop Kontner's Hill in downtown Nelsonville. When it was lighted for the first time in April 1973, it was the world's largest illuminated cross.

The Moonshine Capital
NEW STRAITSVILLE

There's one place in Ohio where it's legal to make moonshine.

Citizens of New Straitsville used to make really good hootch. It's said that during Prohibition, if you walked into a speakeasy in Chicago you might be asked if you wanted a local brand or a "Straitsville Special," it was that good. Today in New Straitsville, many people will boast that an uncle or a father or grandfather ran a still and supported his family during the lean years with bootleg whiskey.

Was it the water in southern Ohio? Or the whiskey-making heritage of the sons and daughters of English, Scotch, Irish, and Welsh immigrants who settled there? One thing's for sure: the hollows, glens, abandoned coal mines, and caves around New Straitsville were perfect for the illicit operation of stills. State and federal liquor-control agents tried to stop them, but the bootleggers were smarter, and some people say that during Prohibition southern Ohio was among the chief suppliers for speakeasies throughout the Midwest. When the "revenuers" came to town, word was passed quickly, and even local folks who didn't drink would help hide the illegal stills.

Prohibition ended nearly 70 years ago, of course, and most stills have long been dismantled. But the folks in New Straitsville don't want to forget. They hold a Moonshine Festival each year around Memorial Day and invite the whole world to watch moonshine being made. State law-enforcement officials allow it under a special permit. And under strict control. Moonshine is made, but they don't sell it, and they don't serve it—not even sipping samples. All you can do is smell it. Then every ounce has to be destroyed under the watchful eye of the state agents.

You *can* consume other things at the five-day festival—moonshine pie and moonshine cookies, for example. A local historian who used to work at the festival said that she put some real, legal whiskey in her moonshine pie—to make it smell and taste like the real thing. She didn't know what goes into the cookies, but guessed it might be a little "sipping whiskey," just enough for flavor.

For information on the Moonshine Festival call the New Straitsville Betterment Association: 740-394-3133.

The Fire that Won't Go Out

NEW STRAITSVILLE

Whatever you do, don't ever tick off a coal miner. Just ask the folks in New Straitsville about the bitter, five-month-long strike between the miners and management back in 1884. The miners were unable to talk management into meeting their demands, and it made them so angry they set the mine on fire. According to historians, the angry miners put timbers in coal cars, soaked them with oil, set them ablaze, and pushed them deep into the mine on Plumber's Hill.

No one could have foreseen how big a fire they were setting.

The blaze started to burn under the ground in the thick, rich deposits of soft Ohio coal. Millions of pounds were destroyed. It is believed that the coal veins were as thick as 14 feet and ran, literally, for miles in all directions.

The fires were so intense that people could draw hot water from their wells and make coffee without a stove. Roads collapsed. Flames shot out of the ground like flaming geysers. The earth around the town started to look like outer space, with smoke and steam escaping from fissures in the earth. The fire crept under the local high school, so weakening the foundation that it had to be closed.

And the fire is still burning beneath New Straitsville after more than 115 years.

There have been several attempts to put it out. During the Great Depression, the federal Works Progress Administration spent $1 million trying to extinguish the burning coal. But there are apparently enough fractures in the rock over the coal that oxygen reaches the smoldering coal and it just keeps on burning. One local historian estimated that the coal has been burning in a 60-square-mile area around New Straitsville.

Sometimes the fire appears to have stopped, showing no evidence of burning for years. But then it breaks out in a new location. The last time was in 1991, when a hole about 15 feet across opened, and smoke and flame belched from the earth. The location, on the edge of the Wayne National Forest, took about three years to burn itself out and disappear back into the earth, where it is probably still smoldering. Some have called the New Straitsville coal fire the "longest-burning manmade fire in history."

You can see historic pictures of the fire and hear some firsthand descriptions of it from members of the New Straitsville History Group (200 W. Main St., New Straitsville; 740-394-2535).

Sometimes the fire appears to
have stopped, showing no evidence
of burning for years. But then it
breaks out in a new location.

The Funniest Intersection in America

WEST CHESTER

The funniest intersection in America is located in Ohio, according to the State Farm Insurance company. The insurance giant researches the most dangerous intersections in America, and they compiled a list of the funniest name combinations they have found. Their number one? The intersection of Grinn and Barrett in West Chester.

The Y Bridge

ZANESVILLE

It's been called the bridge to nowhere. Some people say it just doesn't make much sense, but the Y Bridge in Zanesville has been an Ohio curiosity for nearly two hundred years. It truly is a bridge in the shape of a "Y" that crosses both the Licking and Muskingum rivers. The first version of the bridge was built back in 1814; the present steel and concrete structure is the fifth Y-shaped bridge to be built in this location.

Why the "bridge to nowhere"? Well, this may be the only bridge in the world that you can cross and still end up back on the same side of the river where you started—it's clear if you look at an aerial shot of the bridge.

The Y Bridge is on Route 40 in downtown Zanesville, and you can get a good look at it from on high in nearby Putnam Hill Park.

SOUTHWEST

The Cradle of Dentistry
BAINBRIDGE

The "Cradle of Dentistry" is, according to the Ohio Dental Association, in Bainbridge. There, in 1827, Dr. John Harris opened the first dental school in the U.S. Now it's home to the **John Harris Dental Museum** (open Saturday and Sunday afternoons or by appointment, 208 W. Main St., Bainbridge; 740-634-2228). Exhibits include items used by dentists two hundred years ago that look appropriate for a torture chamber in some dungeon. (Harris's brother, Chapin, also a dentist, was one of the founders of the Baltimore College of Dental Surgery in 1840.)

Flying Saucer Home
CARLISLE

In Carlisle, south of Columbus, passersby at the corner of Central and Chamberlain do a double-take: there sit two flying saucers connected by a silver tube. It's actually a private home.

World's Largest Swimming Pool
CINCINNATI

This swimming pool is so big that the lifeguards have to patrol it from small boats. **Sunlite Pool at Coney Island Park** (6201 Kellogg Ave., Cincinnati; 513-232-8230) near Cincinnati is reported to be the largest recirculating pool in the world—400 feet long and 200 feet wide, holding 3 million gallons of water and accommodating 10,000 swimmers at one time. It also features a 500-foot-long water slide. The depth ranges from six inches to 10 feet.

When the owner decided to build Kings Island Amusement Park north of downtown Cincinnati, many of the Coney Island rides were moved there, and it looked like the end of the road for this riverside attraction. But Cincinnatians wouldn't let it die. They had too many memories of wonderful summers there, and over the years the pool and the associated park have made a comeback. Today, the biggest recirculating pool on earth is again part of a full-fledged amusement park, run by new owners.

Tiny Little Cincinnati
CINCINNATI

They've shrunk downtown Cincinnati to an area about the size of a football field at the **Cincinnati History Museum** (Cincinnati Museum Center, 1301 Western Ave., Cincinnati; 800-733-2077).

It's reproduced at one 64th of its size. The city's skyscraper, the

Carew Tower building, is replicated at a height of about 7 feet.

Miniature cars and trolleys move on the streets, darkness falls, and the lights go on in the city. There is even a vacant lot with a small boy flying a kite and a house that appears to catch fire. You'll feel like Gulliver having his first view of Lilliputian Land when you get your first look at "Cincinnati in Motion." (History moves here also: at the Ohio River side of the city the time is 1940, but as you go away from the river the years drop away until you end in the suburbs in the year 1900.)

The Youngest Player in Professional Baseball
CINCINNATI

Joe Nuxhall was so young when he pitched his first professional baseball game that he had to get special permission from his high school principal. He was just over 15 years old in February of 1944 when the Cincinnati Reds signed him as a pitcher. He had just played a game of high school basketball the night before.

World War II was on at the time, and many of the major and minor league players were in uniform. So to stay alive, professional baseball looked to every source to find players—even high schools.

Nuxhall's big chance came on June 10th of that year when Cincinnati manager Bill McKechnie sent him in to pitch the ninth inning of a game between Cincinnati and the St. Louis Cardinals. He was 15 years, 10 months, and 11 days old, the youngest person to ever play in a game of professional baseball.

He gave up five runs on two hits and five walks and retired two batters.

Following that rather inauspicious beginning, he was sent down to the minors, where he played for seven years. Finally in 1952 he returned to the Reds.

In 1955 he led the league with five shutouts and pitched 3 1/3 scoreless innings in the All-Star Game that year. That was also the year he racked up 17 wins.

His baseball playing days lasted until 1967, when he retired to become a broadcaster for the Cincinnati Reds.

Porker Paradise
EATON

Cincinnati once shipped so many pigs through its river port that it was known the world over as "Porkopolis."

But today that title is better suited to Preble County, home of the **Preble County Pork Festival** (Preble County Fairgrounds, 722 S. Franklin St., Eaton; 937-456-7273), held every year on the third full weekend in September.

Pork farmers here take this festival seriously. There can be as many as 2,500 pork chops on the grill at one time. The Four-H Club sells sugar waffles shaped like pigs. They even have a "Porkville" country store where you can buy fresh pork loin. Sunday after church services they hold several heats of the popular pig races.

The highlight of the festival comes when they put on a sausage-making demonstration. The old-fashioned way. Visitors can actually watch them slaughter a hog, then cut it up and grind up portions to make fresh sausage. (Do the losers of those pig races get chosen to demonstrate the sausage making?)

Little girls are encouraged to wear pigtails, and there is a contest for the best pigtail. The festival's motto is: "The next time you eat a pork chop or see a pig, think of Preble County Pork Festival."

All the Presidents' Planes

FAIRBORN

Dayton has an exhibit that must make other aerospace museums green with envy.

They have four of the five retired primary aircraft dedicated to supporting the president, plus five additional aircraft used by the presidents since World War II.

Dayton is the home of Wright-Patterson Air Force Base, which has the largest and oldest military aviation museum in the world: the **U.S. Air Force Museum** (Wright-Patterson Air Force Base, 1100 Spaatz Ave., Fairborn; 937-255-3286). All airplanes used by the president of the United States are air force planes, so it naturally follows that when they retire, they head for Ohio and the Air Force Museum.

By the time the air force started sending presidential planes to Dayton, the museum there was already crammed with other historical planes. (Its collection now includes a B-52 bomber, a Stealth Fighter, and hundreds of others.) There just wasn't room in the hangar for presidential aircraft, so the planes have been relegated to an old World War II-era hangar that the museum uses for storage.

You can make a reservation to catch the shuttle bus to visit the Presidential Hangar. (Be prepared: the hangars are not air-conditioned and are crowded with many other planes; during the height of the summer tourist season, it can get mighty hot inside.)

Top billing goes to SAM 26000. Does that ring a bell? That big blue-and-silver 707 was used as Air Force One by eight presidents—from John F. Kennedy to Bill Clinton. It holds the distinction of being the aircraft on which Lyndon Johnson was inaugurated as president in 1963 while the plane was on the ground at Love Field in Dallas, shortly after President Kennedy was assassinated.

In addition to Kennedy's Air Force One, you can also see *Columbine III*, the Super Constellation that Dwight Eisenhower used; Harry S. Truman's *Independence*; and the very first presidential airplane, a World War II VC-54C used by Franklin Roosevelt—known as *The Sacred Cow*. (An elevator was installed in the aircraft to get FDR aboard in his wheelchair.)

Admission to the Air Force Museum is free, as is admission to see the presidential aircraft, but you must have a reservation and must use their shuttle bus.

The King of Halloween

FAIRBORN

Time warp! Time warp! That's what your mind will be telling you as you walk into this dime store in Fairborn. The candy case, with its candy corn, root-beer barrels, and bridge mix, is just inside the front door. The floors are wooden and show the passage of time. You can find the traditional things you always found at the dime store: pins and thread, brooms and mops, cards and lace. There's even a pet department where you can buy a small bird. Like all dime stores it's cluttered, with merchandise piled to the ceiling—in some cases its *hanging* from the ceiling.

Foy's Variety Store (18 E. Main St., Fairborn; 937-878-0671) is a Fairborn institution. It was founded in 1929 by Mike Foy, the present owner's grandfather, and remained pretty much unchanged until the last part of the 20th century, when Mike Foy took over.

Mike, you see, *loves* Halloween, and while the dime store had always carried a small selection of Halloween masks and costumes, Mike decided to enlarge the Halloween department. And, boy, did he ever!

Mike Foy has now taken over almost two city blocks in downtown Fairborn, converting former stores into Halloween specialty shops.

One store sells nothing but children's costumes. Another rents and sells costumes for adults. A former bar has been turned into a store for commercial "haunted house" paraphernalia, things like rubber dummies in electric chairs and jail cells with monsters inside fighting to get out. You can buy plastic life-size skeletons here. A former pool hall has been reborn as a diner right out of the 1950s, a neat place to grab a snack while shopping for Halloween goodies.

Last I heard, Mike was negotiating with local realtors for an abandoned granary elevator up the street. "Wouldn't that make a great haunted house?" he asked.

You can't miss Mike's stores when you drive into downtown Fairborn. Just look for the place with the inflatable gorilla on top, next to the one where the skeleton is hanging from the roof. There are also several vintage hearses parked on the street.

The Wacky Grocer

FAIRFIELD

How unusual can a grocery store be? How unusual do you want it? In Fairfield, Jim Bonaminio, known to his customers as "Jungle" Jim, takes great pains to make sure you don't mistake his store—**Jungle Jim's International Market** (5440 Dixie Hwy., Fairfield; 513-674-6000)—for any ordinary one.

For openers, it's big—more than four acres under one roof—but that's not what sets it apart. There's the personality of its owner, Jungle Jim. You can often find him gliding up and down the aisles on roller skates, wearing one of his many costumes. One visit found him dressed as a cowboy on roller skates, with chaps, a western shirt, a hat, and a gun belt. But in the holster, instead of a six-shooter he had a foot-long leek, which he used as a pointer.

And there's entertainment. In the seafood department is a 40-foot cabin cruiser that has seen better days, painted up to be the *S.S. Minnow* and containing an animated band of cartoon characters that break into song every few minutes. There is a singing animatronic Elvis Lion, and a pair of electronic crows that burst into "Rockin' Robin" every five minutes or so.

Against a back wall of the store, past several rows of specialty foods from around the world, there's a small movie theater that continuously plays—what else?—"The Jungle Jim Story: Evolution of the Jungle."

The shelves hold products you won't find in many stores, from water canned from a spring at the base of Mt. Fuji to a box of fresh cactus leaves in the salad department. Jim has become famous for the sheer number of things he carries—more than 110,000 different food items from more than 72 countries. He was among the first grocers to introduce a mushroom bar (like a salad bar, but just for mushrooms).

Oh, yes, and there's the monorail. Jim recently purchased 50 additional acres of land around his store and is building a monorail to circle the property, stopping at markets on the grounds where you'll be able to sample foods from different countries.

Jungle Jim recently purchased 50 additional acres of land around his store and is building a monorail.

Gummy Walls

GREENVILLE

You've been working that big wad of Doublemint in your jaw all morning, and the flavor is finally just about gone. It's lunchtime, and you're pulling up at the **Maid-Rite Sandwich Shop** (125 N. Broadway St., Greenville; 937-548-9340). What to do with the gum? As you head toward the drive-up window, just reach out your window and smack it against the brick building.

Sounds gross, but that's what people have been doing for years. So much so that the walls have taken on the look of a gum sculpture. No one is quite sure just how the custom started, but as they sang in *Fiddler on the Roof*, it's "tradition." Not only don't they scrape it off, they seem to encourage it.

Must help you get your appetite prepared for their featured menu item: "Loose Meat Sandwiches." I'm not exactly sure what "loose meat" means, but an employee said they serve as many as 400 per hour.

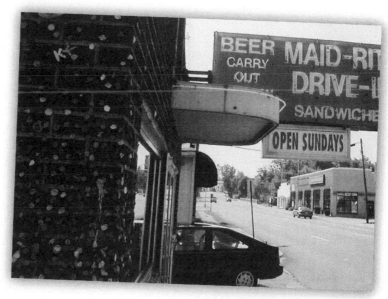

Special on "ABC" gum at the Maid-Rite!
(Gets your juices flowing for the
Loose Meat Sandwich.)

YOU SAY LEE-MA, I SAY LIME-AH

Ohio shares a lot of place names with more famous cities throughout the world. But that doesn't mean we have to pronounce them the same way.

In Peru, Lima is pronounced "Lee-ma." In Ohio, it's "Lime-ah".

There is "Med-eena," Spain and "Med-eye-na," Ohio.

"Mee-lon" is in Italy; "My-lun" is in Ohio.

Most Daltons say it like it looks, but in Ohio it's "Daal-ton."

In Germany it's "Bur-LIN." In most of Ohio we say, "BUR-lin."

Cadiz, Ohio, is pronounced "Cadis," but the one in Spain is "Kah-DIZ."

In the old world, Athens was pronounced "Ath-ens," but in Ohio there is the New "Ay-thens"

By the way, how do you pronounce a town name that only has two letters? Ai, Ohio, would, I guess, be pronounced "A" or "I." For the record, Ai is located in northwest Ohio, in Fulton County.

Mantua trips up news broadcasters in Ohio all the time. It looks like "Man-too-a," but it's pronounced "Mant-a-way."

Folks in "Lo-dye" love it when you don't say "Load-ee" for Lodi.

In Hamilton the local folks got so excited about their town they added an exclamation mark after the name to make sure that everyone knew they were talking about Hamilton! Ohio.

The Hollow Earth Theory

HAMILTON

UFOs don't come from outer space. They come from "inner space"—another world inside of our earth. That, at least, was the pioneering theory of Captain John Cleves Symmes, of Hamilton. The earth, he believed, is not a solid globe; it's made up of concentric spheres and polar voids. In other words, hollow—with large holes at the North and South Poles that would allow access to the inner earth. He also believed people were living there.

Captain Symmes wasn't just somebody's eccentric uncle who went around babbling about strange beliefs. He was a highly respected military officer who had been decorated for bravery in the War of 1812. In his time, he was a respected philosopher. So when he said the earth was hollow, many people listened to him.

Symmes even went so far as to petition Congress to send an expedition to the top of the earth to test his theory and find the hole. While he was unable to convince a majority of Congress to go along with the trip—amazingly, 25 members *did* vote in favor of the expedition—he published the *Symmes Theory of Concentric Spheres* and sent it to educators in America and Europe to help fan the flames of interest in his theory. (In his book, Symmes suggested that the hole in the North Pole was 4,000 miles in diameter; the hole in the South Pole was 6,000 miles in diameter.)

Even after Peary's discovery of the North Pole (with no sign of an accompanying 4,000-mile-in-diameter hole), many people still believed in Symmes's theories. Even today there are still proponents of the Hollow Earth theory.

In Hamilton, at least, there *are* holes at the ends of the earth—atop the Symmes memorial statue, in a park located between Third and Fourth streets.

In his time, he was a respected philosopher. So when he said the earth was hollow, many people listened to him.

Pyramid Hill Sculpture Park

HAMILTON

Harry T. Wilks, a retired attorney from Hamilton, likes his art BIG. Wilks bought 45 acres of wooded land for a home and built a beautiful underground home in the side of a hill. Then he bought more land. And then he got the idea to build a park for sculptures. Not just any sculptures—really *big* sculptures. Thus **Pyramid Hill Sculpture Park** (State Rte. 128, Hamilton; 513-868-8336) was born. He kept on buying adjoining land adding up to 265 acres of hilly property.

Today at this non-profit arts and cultural center, there are more than three dozen enormous works of art placed on hills and in valleys. The largest is *Abracadabra*, by Alexander Liberman. The vast, twisted red metal sculpture is two-and-a-half stories tall and nearly four stories wide. Pilots landing at nearby Cincinnati Regional Airport have said they can easily see it from the air.

The Serpent Mound

LOCUST GROVE

One of Ohio's best-known mysteries is the Serpent Mound in the southern part of the state.

Nearly a quarter of a mile long, the mound lies on a plateau in the valley of Brush Creek, near Hillsboro. Historians believe it was built by the Adena Indians about 2,000 years ago, but since there is no written history of that culture, no one is sure.

The mound, an earthen ridge about three feet high that twists and turns for more than 1,330 feet, gets its name from the fact that from above it looks like an uncoiling serpent with an egg in its mouth. While no evidence of burials has been found in the Serpent Mound, nearby conical mounds did contain bodies of the Adena people dating back to around 800 B.C.

Why the Serpent Mound was built has always puzzled investigators. It might have been for religious rites, or as sort of an early calendar (in conjunction with the movement of the moon and stars).

Today you can best see the **Serpent Mound** (3850 State Rte. 73, Locust Grove; 800-752-2757) from an observation tower on the grounds.

A Man's Castle is His Home

LOVELAND

In 1973, Harry Andrews, who never married and had no family, decided to start a band of knights. Conveniently, he already had his own castle.

The dream actually started in Loveland right after the first world war. Andrews had just returned from Europe enchanted by the wondrous sights he had seen—especially the castles in England and France. He daydreamed about them for years—until 1927, when he decided to make his fantasy come true.

He taught Sunday school to a group of teenagers. He would occasionally take them to a favorite swimming hole along the Little Miami River. Here the class would camp out, fish and swim. Andrews eventually bought the property and challenged the youngsters to help him build what he originally called "a stone tent."

The kids helped carry buckets of stones and sand from the river to the construction site. Two small stone rooms were completed by

1929, just as the Great Depression swept the country. As hard times moved across Ohio, many of the youngsters were sent off to work in the Civilian Conservation Corps; work on the building slowed. And as some families broke up due to lack of work and money, Andrews found himself caring for some of the youngsters who used to be in his Sunday school class. He would regale them with stories of the great castles he had seen during his wartime service. As the Depression eased, Andrews had a new vision: his "stone tents" would become the base of his very own castle, and to build that castle he would seek the help of anyone who shared his dream.

Bucket by bucket of stones and sand, the castle grew over the next 30 years. He gave it a name, **Chateau La Roche** (12025 Shore Dr., Loveland; 513-683-4686)—"house of stone." Today it's a three-story castle surrounded by four-story-high battle towers. And most of the work was done by one man: Harry Andrews.

The castle walls are 30 inches thick, built with handmade concrete bricks formed from the rocks and sand that people carried from the nearby river. Many of the forms for the bricks were old paper milk cartons that neighbors would donate. Inside, the stairways to the upper floors are built so only one person at a time can go up the stairs, making defense of the second floor easier. The two-cell dungeon was used by Andrews to store jams and jellies that he would put up each fall.

In the 1950s, Andrews gave up his job at a publishing foundation and devoted the rest of his life to working on the castle. Eventually he discovered that without meaning to, he had created a tourist attraction. Frequently while he was working alone on the building, carloads of the curious would stop by and ask questions or want to take pictures. By the late 1970s, upwards of 50,000 people per year were stopping by. Something had to be done.

That's when Andrews incorporated the Knights of the Golden Trail and directed that upon his death that the knights would take over ownership of the castle and grounds.

Monument to a Pig
MIDDLETOWN

Just outside of Middletown is a tribute to a pig. Not just *a* pig, actually, but a whole race of pigs. Namely, the Poland China Hog.

It was on a farm here that the very first Poland China Hog in the nation was bred and born. The breed was so successful that today Poland China Hogs are popular all over the world. A six-foot-tall stone monument to the hog was erected near the original farm. (A shopping mall was erected *on* the farm, but you can still see the memorial across from the entrance to Towne Mall on Route 25 if you look carefully.)

For more information about the hog statue, try the Middletown Historical Society (56 S. Main St., Middletown; 513-424-5539).

The Missing Body
NORTH BEND

Ohio has a lot of presidential stories. After all, the state competes with Virginia for the title "Mother of Presidents." But there is one presidential story that is rarely told, involving a man who was the son of one U.S. president and the father of another.

John Scott Harrison was the son of the first U.S. President from Ohio, William Henry Harrison (who holds the record for the shortest term of office: he died after being in office only 30 days), and the father of Benjamin Harrison.

John Scott died at the age of 74 in 1878. It was a time when doctors were not allowed to use human remains to practice on, so the grim business of grave robbing was relied on to supply medical schools. Grave robbers closely watched the obituaries in the paper, then snuck into a cemetery after a funeral to dig up the fresh body.

The Harrison family, aware of this danger, took precautions when they buried John Scott in the North Bend cemetery. His grave contained a cemented brick vault, and after his casket was lowered into it, it was covered with logs and stones to make removal difficult.

A week after Harrison was buried, his family heard that the body of a neighbor, Augustus Devin, was missing from the same cemetery. Suspecting that nearby medical schools were responsible, the Harrison family led a posse into Cincinnati. At the Medical College of Ohio, they discovered a hidden trap door and, behind it, a nude body hanging upside down by a rope.

When they pulled the sheet from the face of the cadaver, the Harrisons found themselves staring not at their neighbor but at their own father, John Scott Harrison. They later found the body of Augustus Devin in a pickle barrel filled with brine.

The discovery and the resulting publicity across the country led to a change in laws allowing medical schools to use donated and unclaimed bodies for scientific purposes. It finally brought an end to grave robbing.

As for John Scott Harrison, his family reinterred him in the vault with his father, William Henry Harrison, behind barred doors and with no marker on whichever crypt held his body. You can still see the tomb of both Harrisons in North Bend, overlooking the Ohio River.

For information contact the Ohio Historical Society (1982 Velma Ave., Columbus; 614-297-2300).

Home of Underwear Greatness

PIQUA

A historical marker just outside Piqua commemorates Don Gentile, World War II Army Air Force fighter ace, as the local hero. But the rest of the world probably knows Piqua best as the home of a *super-hero*: Captain Underpants.

Dav Pilkey, author of the *Captain Underpants* children's book series (most popular with the fourth-grade crowd), wrote "I chose Piqua because they have an Underwear Festival there every year. It seemed like the perfect place!"

Sadly, they *used* to have an Underwear Festival. But no more. The festival hasn't been held in recent years because of declining attendence, reported the Piqua Chamber of Commerce.

Why did Piqua celebrate underwear in the first place? It's the birthplace of the union suit, that red, one-piece longjohn with the flap in the seat—invented locally by the Atlas Underwear Company (or possibly one of eight other competing underwear companies operating in Piqua during the early part of the 20th Century—they all took credit for it at one time or another).

General Grant's Wandering Home
POINT PLEASANT

Ohio has a wealth of presidential history. Maybe that's why we're a bit casual with some of our historic sites. Take Ulysses S. Grant's birthplace, a tiny cottage on the Ohio River at Point Pleasant in Clermont County.

To be fair, Grant was born here and lived in the building for less than a year before the family moved on to a bigger home in nearby Georgetown. But it was still his birthplace, and those sorts of things are usually kept track of, at least for presidents.

Not much was ever made of the place until after Grant had helped win the Civil War and served as president of the United States. Then, in the late 1800s, enterprising souls decided to make a buck on the birthplace. They put it on a large barge and floated it up and down the Ohio, Missouri, and Mississippi rivers, charging admission to see the actual house where Grant was born.

Then, if that wasn't indignity enough, in the 1920s the little building was torn down, loaded on flatcars, and taken to Columbus, where it was reconstructed as an exhibit at the Ohio State Fair. The building got pretty shabby from lack of attention during the Great Depression until in 1936 it was rescued, taken down again, returned to Point Pleasant, and reconstructed on its original foundation.

Today **President Grant's birthplace** (U.S. Rte. 52, Point Pleasant; 513-553-4911) is on the National Register of Historic Places, and that should keep it in one place for a while.

Leonard Slye from Duck Run

PORTSMOUTH

Ohio can claim to be the birthplace of at least two kings: "King of Hollywood" Clark Gable (see "A King Was Born Here," Cadiz) and "King of the Cowboys" Roy Rogers.

Rogers was crowned king through a bit of press-agent gimmickry during World War II, when rival singing cowboy Gene Autry was serving in the U.S. Air Force and unable to make movies.

Rogers was America's most popular cowboy at the box office for 12 straight years. He made more than 80 movies. He recorded songs and made television appearances—there were books and comic books, furniture, lunch buckets, toys, you-name-it, stamped with his name and likeness.

Heady stuff for a guy who started out as Leonard Frank Slye from Cincinnati, Ohio. He spent his childhood in a community called Duck Run, in Scioto County near Portsmouth. It was from here that his family packed up and decided to move to California during the Great Depression.

Roy's Cincinnati birthplace was torn down years ago to make way for Cynergy Field, but you can still see the home he grew up in near Portsmouth (though it is a private residence and there are no tours).

In downtown Portsmouth there is the Roy Rogers Esplanade, with a concrete slab that contains Rogers's footprints and handprints from a public appearance he once made in town.

The Shoelace Capital
PORTSMOUTH

If you wear shoelaces, chances are they were made in Ohio. Portsmouth is home to the the world's largest manufacturer of shoelaces.

Now you might think a shoelace factory isn't a big deal, but **Mitchellace, Inc.** (830 Murray St., Portsmouth; 740-354-2813) occupies a 360,000-square-foot factory. The plant, several stories high and covering a city block, produces more than four million pairs of shoelaces every week.

Ah, pairs. Did you know that you can't buy just one shoe-string? That marketing gimmick was started many years ago by Mitchellace (which has been around since 1902). They pack two laces to a package so you always have to buy an extra one.

Aunt Jemima Was Once a Buckeye
RIPLEY

Aunt Jemima wasn't a real person, just an advertising gimmick to sell self-rising pancake flour. But real people were hired to portray her. The first was Nancy Green, hired in 1893 at the Columbian Exposition in Chicago to wear a bandanna on her head and make and promote the pancakes. After she died in an auto accident in 1923, Quaker Oats started hiring other women to promote the pancake mix. One of these was Rosa "Rosie" Riles of Ripley. Riles was tapped to portray Aunt Jemima in ads, and she also made personal appearances all through Ohio, Indiana, Illinois, and Kentucky. She died in 1969 and is buried in the Red Oak Presbyterian Church cemetery, near Ripley. The church has a small exhibit on Riles's career as Aunt Jemima.

Smoke, Smoke, Smoke

RIPLEY

Got someone in the family who just can't live without lighting up? Someone who refuses to go to a restaurant that doesn't allow smoking? Here's the place for them.

The **Ohio Tobacco Festival** (937-373-3651) is held in Ripley, usually in late August.

There's a lot of tobacco grown in southern Ohio, and this is one place where smoking is definitely allowed.

The festival includes tobacco worm races, a tobacco stripping and plugging contest, a garden-tractor obstacle race, and—fun for the whole family—a tobacco spitting contest.

Can't get enough smoke at the festival? Try the **Ohio Tobacco Festival Museum** (703 S. Second St., Ripley; 937-392-9410).

The Man Who Built a Roller Coaster

ROSS

You have to admire Ralph Stricker. He's one of those single-minded people who make their minds up to do something and won't let anything or anyone stop them. Not even his wife.

Ralph wanted to build a roller coaster in his cornfield.

He doesn't particularly like to *ride* roller coasters, mind you, but he had always been fascinated by the way the big wooden coasters were put together, almost like a giant jigsaw puzzle.

Ralph worked most of his adult life at Procter & Gamble as a stationary engineer. He was also a pretty fair self-taught carpenter.

As he neared retirement, he would go to amusement parks like Kings Island, but instead of riding the roller coasters, he would just stand and study them from many different angles. He eventually talked one of the coaster designers at the park into helping him design his own.

In May of 1990, Ralph Stricker and two helpers started building a wooden coaster in his former cornfield. He called it the Tornado. The work went on summer and winter. Ralph and his helpers hauled long timbers to their barn so they could build "bents," the legs of wooden roller coasters. From an old amusement park in Florida he obtained the chains and gears to work the ride. He finally bought new cars from the Philadelphia Toboggan Company, the firm that specializes in roller-coaster cars.

In June of 1993, Ralph finally stood atop his highest hill. The coaster, 55 feet tall and 2,080 long, was done.

To a real coaster fan, used to two- and three-hundred-foot drops, that might seem pretty tame. But Ralph Stricker built this one himself.

I had a chance to ride Ralph's "Tornado" once. While it may not compete with Kings Island's The Beast or Cedar Point's Magnum, it's a good, solid wooden coaster that gives a decent ride and even a little airtime (little hills that launch you out of your seat for a second or two). I was having a great time, but when I looked over my shoulder at Ralph, who was riding behind me, he had no expression on his face at all. I asked him later if he was enjoying himself, and he replied, "I just build 'em, I don't ride 'em."

In fact, Ralph enjoyed building the "Tornado" so much that the next year he started building a second roller coaster, a scaled-down version called the "Teddy Bear."

Ralph Stricker decided to build it whether they come or not, for the sheer pleasure of creating his very own roller coaster.

Stricker's Grove (11490 Hamilton-Cleves Rd./Ohio Rte. 128, Ross; 513-738-3366), which has Ralph's roller coaster and a dozen or so other mechanical rides, is open for corporate rentals during the summer and open to the public on only two days, the Fourth of July and the second Sunday in August.

The Legend of Eugene

SABINA

Sabina is located in the northeastern part of Clinton County. One of the slogans they have used over the years is "1,700 friendly people welcome you to Sabina."

It may have been that sign that attracted Eugene to Sabina back in June of 1929. He might also have just been passing through, a man from nowhere, going nowhere. Sadly, no one will ever know.

The good folks of Sabina had their first encounter with Eugene on the morning of June 6, when the body of an African-American male was discovered along Highway 3C, near Borum Road.

Dr. C. E. Kinzel, the county coroner, was called. He determined that the body was that of a man 50 to 60 years old and that he apparently had died of "natural causes." The only piece of identification on the body was a slip of paper that said, "1118 Yale Avenue, Cincinnati, Ohio." There was no name. Local officers immediately alerted the Cincinnati police, who drove to the address, only to find a vacant lot.

They told Sabina authorities that they had questioned the man living nearest to the vacant lot, a Eugene Johnson, who told them he had no knowledge of a missing man in his neighborhood and did not recognize the description of the dead body in Sabina.

For some reason officials in Sabina, using this information, gave the body the nickname "Eugene."

Not knowing what to do with the body, the local police had it transferred to Littleton Funeral Home in Sabina to have it embalmed. Days went by, then weeks and months. No missing persons reports were received that matched Eugene's description.

Finally, in desperation, Sabina authorities decided to place Eugene's body on display in a small brick building near the funeral home, in hopes that some visitor might recognize him and they would be able to reunite him with his family.

By this time, Eugene, in death, had become quite a local celebrity. As word spread about the mysterious body, people came from all over to view the remains, which by this time had been spruced up with a new suit of clothes.

Well, you know how things go in a small town. People got busy with one thing or another, and while they didn't exactly forget about Eugene, he just sort of became part of the town. Next thing you know, 35 years had gone by with Eugene living, so to speak, in his little brick building, being stared at by tourists and people passing through the town who had heard of the legend. He was viewed by an estimated 1.3 million visitors, but no one ever recognized him.

About the only time Eugene ever got any publicity in those days was when high school or college pranksters would "borrow" him, take him to some nearby town, and place him on a park bench, where he would stay until he was found and the funeral home was called to come and take him back home.

It was an increase in this kind of prank, and the fact that 35 years had passed without anybody identifying him, that finally prompted the Littleton family to put an end to the story. Deciding they had done everything they could to identify him, they purchased a tombstone and a plot in the Sabina Cemetery (330 N. College St., Sabina) and finally had Eugene laid to rest.

His tombstone reads: "'Eugene' found dead 1928 [this is an error, it was 1929] buried 1964."

Creating the World with a Hammer
SPRINGFIELD

Ben Hartman of Springfield just wanted to build a small fishpond in his backyard. It was the Great Depression, and he was out of work and wanted to keep busy. But that small cement-and-stone fishpond grew into an obsession that kept him building the rest of his life.

After the fishpond, he decided to build a miniature version of the "Little Church Around the Corner," the famous New York City landmark. Then he decided to build a small replica of a country schoolhouse. After that, said his widow, Mary Hartman, he just "always seemed to be working on something, he had all these ideas."

Christ on Calvary joined the Barbara Fritchie home (where she defied Stonewall Jackson). Independence Hall in Philadelphia was built near Flander Field from the First World War.

Hartman got the stones to build his world from a nearby housing development where fields were being cleared of rocks. He'd bring them back to his workshop and break them into small pieces with a hammer. In seven years he wore out three hammers.

He built a four-foot-high stone cup and saucer. He created a replica in stone of the birthplace of Abraham Lincoln. There was Custer's Last Stand, and Noah's Ark.

When curious neighbors and passersby who had heard of the project would stop over, Hartman would stop working and show them around. If someone pressed a coin into his hand when they left, he would save it until he had enough to buy another bag of cement and build some more. He even built a castle eight feet high and six feet wide, complete with moat and drawbridge. It took 14,000 stones to do that.

In all, Ben Hartman crushed up a quarter of a million stones, one at a time, to build his hundreds and hundreds of statues, figures, and buildings.

Ben Hartman died a long time ago, in 1944, and time has eroded some of his little world. But Mary still plants flowers around her yard and welcomes strangers who want to see what one man and three hammers could accomplish.

The Hartman Rock Garden is on the corner of McKaw and Russell streets in Springfield. According to the Springfield Vistors' Bureau (937-325-7621), visitors are welcome. Hours are whenever someone is at home.

What Time Is It?
UNION CITY

What time is it? That's a simple question, unless you're in Union City. Then it depends on which side of the street you live on.

You see, Union City, Ohio, and Union City, Indiana, share a lot of things, including the Ohio-Indiana border. It looks like one small town, but it acts like two. They have two city halls, two police and fire departments, and even two school systems.

But what really sets them apart is Daylight Savings Time. Ohio uses it, but Indiana doesn't, remaining on Eastern Standard Time. So summertime in Union City can get a bit confusing, even for long-time residents.

For example, anyone advertising a local event must specify the time in both Ohio and Indiana times if they hope to attract a crowd on time. Taverns on the Ohio side of the line have to close an hour earlier than their counterparts just a block away. Heck, some people who walk to their jobs leave home nearly an hour after they get to work. Huh?

Ohio's "Most Perfect Tree"
WAVERLY

Waverly claims to be the home of perfection. Specifically, Ohio's "most perfect tree." The 200-year-old hard maple is the lead item in the local tourist bureau's brochure.

No one is quite sure just who first noticed that the tree was perfect.

"Old-timers here swear they have always known," wrote Linda Basye, who runs the Pike County Convention and Visitors Bureau (12455 State Rte. 104, Waverly; 740-947-9650). "But no paperwork has turned up, aside from some early newspaper clippings that also refer to it as 'Ohio's Perfect Tree.'"

She suspects that the designation dates back to the late 1800s, when Pike County had some political influence in the state.

The tree is located on State Route 355, just 3 1/2 miles south of the intersection with State Route 32. It's on private property, but the Ohio Department of Transportation has thoughtfully carved out a three-car parking area from which the tree can easily be seen.

The First Banana Split

WILMINGTON

Turf wars have erupted over some pretty silly things through the years. Like, who has the biggest ball of string? Or, where was the first cheeseburger cooked? But when they start talking about ice cream, one thing's for sure: Ohio is the birthplace of the banana split.

The good folks in Wilmington have been making that claim since the beginning of the last century. It was old "Doc" Hazard at Hazard's Drug Store who one day decided to add a banana to a rather large ice-cream sundae. He wanted to make it look even bigger, so he cut the banana lengthwise into two pieces and called it a "banana split."

Disregard the folks in Latrobe, Pennsylvania, who are "Johnny-come-latelys" to the banana split wars. They claim the dessert was invented in a drug store in their town in 1905, but by the time they announced this, Wilmington had already put in its claim for the honor, citing 1907 as the date the delicacy was first created.

To cement their claim, Wilmington holds a Banana Split Festival each year on the second weekend in June, and thousands of people flock to the town to sample a banana split the way it was made back in 1907. For information, call the Clinton County Convention and Visitors' Bureau (877-428-4748). **Gibson's Goodies** (718 Ohio Ave., Wilmington; 937-383-2373) claims to have the original banana split recipe.

A slice of history: the original banana split recipe, according to Gibson Goodies in Wilmington.

ACKNOWLEDGMENTS

There aren't enough words to say thank-you to all the folks who helped make this book possible. I do want to pay tribute here to some of the folks who went above and beyond and over and above and all those good things to help me.

From Tim Wrenn, of Sandusky, who dragged me around the Lake Erie Islands in his brand new boat so I could get a close-up picture of the "Benson Ford" the incredible boat-home on the shores of South Bass Island. To my good friend and talented author and journalist, Carl Feather of Ashtabula, who told me the story of the headless rooster of Ashtabula and was kind enough to search through his own manuscripts and records to let me see the original story he had written on the incident. He was also kind enough to share several other ideas that made it into the book. There was also David Giffles, the popular and talented columnist with the *Akron Beacon-Journal* who also was kind enough to give me space several times in his columns and to urge his readers to send me their most curious and weirdest stories. (One of his readers suggested his whole family would qualify as weird!) Thanks to them we uncovered the story of Queen Victoria's underpants in the Kent State University Museum, and David reminded me of the specialness of the historic Akron Dirigible Airdock, along with many other ideas.

Richard Rolenz of Akron for the tip on the hearing aid museum at Kent State University, and Bob Hines in Columbus for suggesting the story of "Chic-Chic," the chicken who bought his own lunch.

Historian, Dr. Roger Bridges, Curator Jay Snider and Thomas Culbertson of the Hayes Presidential Center in Fremont for answering countless questions and doing it with great patience, even when they were busy with other things. I also appreciate their suggestions for some of the presidential items that appear in this book, as well as helping me separate fact from fiction on some items.

Historian and author Richard McElroy of the McKinley Museum and National Memorial in Canton for helping me confirm the story about McKinley's carnation in "Don't give away your good luck charm", as well as his many other suggestions for the book.

My appreciation to Cathi Baumgardner of the Ohio State Fair for tracking down the picture of the butter cow for me.

Longtime friends, Ted and Karen Driscol, of Lorain, who helped in the early stages of research with trips to the library and several suggestions.

To my bosses at Fox 8 TV, Mike Renda, Greg Easterly and Kevin Salyer, for all their patience and understanding, and most of all for never asking me "Where are you going this week?"

My colleagues Cragg Eichman, Mark Saksa, Jimmy Holloway, Bob Wilkinson, Ralph Tarsitano, Gregg Lockhart, Roger Powell, Loren Kruse, and Bill Wolfe, for their assistance in taking and getting some of the pictures in this book.

To former *Ohio Motorist* Editor Bill Johnson for his editorial advice and guidance in the beginning of my research.

One person I especially want included here is my colleague at Fox 8 TV, Lisa March. Lisa has been responsible for all of my recent half-hour One Tank Trip specials and she brings to each show her energy, enthusiasm and wonderful journalistic skills and shares them with me, while I get all the credit, and she does most of the work.

As I write this I am aware that I will probably overlook others who made equally valuable contributions to the making of this book and to those whom I forgot, my apologies, I hope you will remind me so that we can include you in future editions.

To be sure it would be impossible to thank every single person who contributed to this book. There were literally hundreds, and I hope you all know that I am grateful for the help.

Two other people that help make the TV version of "One Tank Trips" possible, who have also contributed ideas and suggestions for *Ohio Oddities*, are Steve Goldurs, the man who does the video-tape editing of my weekly segments, and Bob Levkulich, our talented graphics director at Fox8 TV.

My daughter and son-in-law, Peter and Melissa Luttmann, my wife, Bonnie, and son, Craig, for supplying some of the pictures that I was unable to get to. To my other daughter and son in law, Melody and Ernie McCallister, for their suggestions and encouragement in writing this book.

Photo Credits

Photographs by the author except: p. 17, courtesy of Circleville Pumpkin Show; p. 20, courtesy of Ohio State Fair; p. 22, courtesy of Dewberry Mudboggers Lawnmower Racing Team; p. 30, courtesy of *The Marion Star*; p. 34 (both), courtesy of Marion County Historical Society; p. 37, courtesy of The Longaberger Company; p. 40, courtesy of The American Ceramic Society; p. 47, courtesy of Rutherford B. Hayes Presidential Center; p. 51, courtesy of Allen County Museum; p. 57, courtesy of ; p. 63, courtesy of Ohio Division of Travel & Tourism; p. 69, courtesy of The Crowne Plaza Akron at Quaker Square; p. 73, courtesy of *Ashtabula Star Beacon;* p. 80, courtesy of Wolf Timbers; p. 85, Dave Hopper; p. 97, courtesy of The Cleveland Museum of Natural History; pp. 100, 102, courtesy of Cleveland Police Historical Society and Museum; p. 110, courtesy of Health Museum of Cleveland; p. 123, Kevin Ruic; p. 125, Harry Cameron; p. 126, courtesy of Kent State University Fashion Museum; p. 129, courtesy of Columbia Career Center; p. 144, courtesy of Hoover Historical Center; pp. 145, 146, Bonnie Zurcher; p. 153, courtesy of Twinsburg Twins Day Festival; p. 155, Dick Goddard; p. 161, courtesy of Vernon Craig; p. 173, courtesy of Athens County Convention and Visitors' Bureau; p. 174, courtesy of New Straitsville Moonshine Festival; p. 182, courtesy of Preble County Pork Festival; p. 183, courtesy of U.S. Air Force Museum; p. 186, courtesy of Jungle Jim's International Farmer's Market; p. 187, courtesy of Greenville/Darke County Convention and Visitors' Bureau; p. 191, Melissa Luttman; p. 198, Roger Powell; p. 203, courtesy of Seville Historical Society; p. 204, courtesy of Pike County Convention and Visitors' Bureau.

INDEX

About the Author

Neil Zurcher, an Emmy-award-winning reporter for Fox8 TV in Cleveland, has reported on unusual travel destinations for more than 20 years. His popular "One Tank Trips" reports are the longest-running local travel segment on television.

He also writes regularly for *AAA Ohio Motorist* magazine and is the author of three other books: *Neil Zurcher's Favorite One Tank Trips*, *More of Neil Zurcher's One Tank Trips*, and *One Tank Trips Road Food*.

Zurcher received the Distinguished Service award from the Society of Professional Journalism and the "Silver Circle" award from the National Academy of Television Arts and Sciences. Former Governor of Ohio George Voinovich called him "One of the most respected and knowledgeable travel writers in the state."

Did I Miss Something?

Well, that's what second editions are for. If I left out your favorite Ohio Oddity, or if you know of someplace in the book that has changed, please let me know; I'll try to include it next time I update the book. Write to me at:

Ohio Oddities
c/o Gray & Company, Publishers
1588 E. 40th St.
Cleveland, OH 44103

email: ohiooddities@grayco.com